Timothy and Titus

The StoryChanger Devotional Series

By David Murray

Exodus: Stories of Redemption and Relationship
Proverbs: Stories of Wisdom and Folly
Luke: Stories of Mission and Mercy
Philippians and Colossians: Stories of Joy and Identity
Timothy and Titus: Stories of Fear and Courage

"We are created for stories. We read stories, tell stories, watch stories, and live in stories. Yet we instinctively know and long for our stories to fit into something bigger, more meaningful, and more comprehensive. As we read Scripture, we can see how that longing might be fulfilled, but we don't always know how to connect our own stories to the great story of redemption that culminates with Christ. This is why I'm so thankful for David Murray's StoryChanger series. These short devotionals are wonderful guides for connecting our stories with God's larger story and helping us call others into God's great story. I gladly recommend their use in personal, family, and group prayer and devotional settings."

Chris Bruno, Global Partner for Hawaii and the Pacific Islands, Training Leaders International; author, *The Whole Story of the Bible in 16 Verses*

"David Murray's new StoryChanger Devotional series is exactly what Christians are craving right now. These daily devotionals are accessible both in their content and brevity. In just a few minutes each day, readers will find comfort in the truth of the gospel and challenges in following the way of Jesus. Just because the devotionals are short doesn't mean that they won't pack a life-changing punch. This series will introduce you to the Bible in the ways that you want and provoke you in the ways that you need."

Adam Griffin, coauthor, *Family Discipleship*; Host, *The Family Discipleship Podcast*; Pastor, Eastside Community Church, Dallas, Texas

"What I appreciate most about the StoryChanger Devotional series is how accessible it is to a wide range of ages. Whether you read these books alone or with others, you'll find them to be practical, easy to follow, and helpful for applying the truths of Scripture to your everyday life. My family enjoys using the StoryChanger Devotionals for our Bible reading and discussion time. The readings prompt encouraging discussions about Scripture around our dinner table each night."

Glenna Marshall, author, *The Promise Is His Presence* and *Everyday Faithfulness*

"We live in a world that takes pride in technological progress. And yet here we are, still a people shaped by stories—our own, those presented to us by the world, and those handed down to us by history. In the StoryChanger Devotional series David Murray has crafted brief, engaging, and accessible devotions based on the biblical text. Each volume will help us understand God's story, make sense of the world around us and, along the way, discover the transformation we need in our personal story. Slow down a while, open your Bible, and let these books prompt your ponderings about God's story and yours."

Peter Mead, Pastor, Trinity Chippenham, United Kingdom; Director, Cor Deo; blogger, BiblicalPreaching.net

"If you are looking for biblically based devotional books that are surprisingly accessible to any level of Christian maturity, you have picked the right series. The StoryChanger Devotional series is uniquely useful because David Murray wrote it. He has a special writing gift that demonstrates his skill as an expositor and his shepherding intuition as a pastor. That gift is wonderfully present in every volume, and I commend this whole series to pastors to buy in bulk and distribute to your entire congregation to study together."

Brian Croft, Executive Director, Practical Shepherding

Timothy and Titus

Stories of Fear and Courage

David Murray

WHEATON, ILLINOIS

Timothy and Titus: Stories of Fear and Courage
© 2024 by David Murray
Published by Crossway
        1300 Crescent Street
        Wheaton, Illinois 60187
All rights reserved. No part of this publication may be reproduced, stored in a retrieval system, or transmitted in any form by any means, electronic, mechanical, photocopy, recording, or otherwise, without the prior permission of the publisher, except as provided for by USA copyright law. Crossway® is a registered trademark in the United States of America.

Published in association with the literary agency of Legacy, LLC, 501 N. Orlando Avenue, Suite #313-348, Winter Park, FL 32789

Cover image and design: Jordan Singer

First printing 2024

Printed in the United States of America

Scripture quotations are from the ESV® Bible (The Holy Bible, English Standard Version®), © 2001 by Crossway, a publishing ministry of Good News Publishers. Used by permission. All rights reserved. The ESV text may not be quoted in any publication made available to the public by a Creative Commons license. The ESV may not be translated into any other language.

Trade paperback ISBN: 978-1-4335-8105-2
ePub ISBN: 978-1-4335-8108-3
PDF ISBN: 978-1-4335-81006-9

Library of Congress Cataloging-in-Publication Data

Names: Murray, David, 1966– author.
Title: Timothy and Titus : stories of fear and courage / David Murray.
Description: Wheaton, Illinois : Crossway, [2024] | Series: The storychanger devotional series | Includes bibliographical references.
Identifiers: LCCN 2023005474 (print) | LCCN 2023005475 (ebook) | ISBN 9781433581052 (trade paperback) | ISBN 9781433581069 (pdf) | ISBN 9781433581083 (epub)
Subjects: LCSH: Bible Timothy—Criticism, interpretation, etc. | Bible Titus—Criticism, interpretation, etc. | Fear—Religious Aspects—Christianity.
Classification: LCC BS2745.2 .M87 2024 (print) | LCC BS2745.2 (ebook) | DDC 227/.830—dc23/eng/20230706
LC record available at https://lccn.loc.gov/2023005474
LC ebook record available at https://lccn.loc.gov/2023005475

Crossway is a publishing ministry of Good News Publishers.

VP		33	32	31	30	29	28	27	26	25	24
15	14	13	12	11	10	9	8	7	6	5	4	3	2	1

*To Jean Gomes.
My copastor, brother, and friend.*

Contents

Introduction to the StoryChanger Devotionals   1

Introduction to *Timothy and Titus: Stories of Fear and Courage*   5

1 TIMOTHY

1. Fighting for Love (1 Timothy 1:1–5)   9
2. Theological Terrorists (1 Timothy 1:6–11)   13
3. Christ Trusts the Untrustworthy with His Trustworthy Gospel (1 Timothy 1:11–12)   17
4. Great Sin, Great Salvation, And Great Service (1 Timothy 1:13–17)   21
5. Delivered to Satan (1 Timothy 1:18–20)   25
6. The Prayer Pivot (1 Timothy 2:1–3)   29
7. Our "All People" Savior (1 Timothy 2:3–4)   33
8. The Limits of an Unlimited Salvation (1 Timothy 2:5–7)   37
9. Male Sins (1 Timothy 2:8)   41
10. What Is a Beautiful Woman? (1 Timothy 2:9–10)   45

11	A Revolutionary Role for Women (1 Timothy 2:11–15)	49
12	Christlike Leadership (1 Timothy 3:1–7)	53
13	Table-Waiters Required (1 Timothy 3:8–13)	57
14	Creeds Need Churches and Churches Need Creeds (1 Timothy 3:14–16)	61
15	Will He Hold Me Fast? (1 Timothy 4:1–5)	65
16	God's Healthcare Plan (1 Timothy 4:6–8)	69
17	The Real Reason We Don't Evangelize (1 Timothy 4:9–10)	73
18	An Inspiring Call to Young Christians (1 Timothy 4:11–16)	77
19	Four Skills in Personal Relationships (1 Timothy 5:1–2)	81
20	God's Heart for the Poor (1 Timothy 5:3–16)	85
21	The Pros and Cons of Leadership (1 Timothy 5:17–25)	89
22	Witnessing at Work (1 Timothy 6:1–2)	93
23	Fake News That's Fatal News (1 Timothy 6:3–5)	97
24	Get-Rich-Slowly Scheme (1 Timothy 6:6–8)	101
25	A Good Friend Becomes Our Worst Enemy (1 Timothy 6:8–10)	105
26	The Four F's of the Christian Life (1 Timothy 6:11–12)	109
27	God the Master-Motivator (1 Timothy 6:12–14)	113
28	Winning by Worshiping (1 Timothy 6:15–16)	117
29	The Pros and Cons of Being Rich (1 Timothy 6:17–21)	121

2 TIMOTHY

30	Look Back to Look Forward (2 Timothy 1:1–7)	127

31	Suffering without Shame (2 Timothy 1:8–18)	*131*
32	Sustainable and Affordable Energy (2 Timothy 2:1–7)	*135*
33	Three Therapeutic Thoughts (2 Timothy 2:8–13)	*139*
34	Our Fatal Attraction (2 Timothy 2: 14–19)	*143*
35	Spiritual Olympics (2 Timothy 2:20–26)	*147*
36	Our Messed-Up World (2 Timothy 3:1–9)	*151*
37	Mentoring Matters (2 Timothy 3:10–17)	*155*
38	The Greatest Blessing Can Be the Worst Curse (2 Timothy 4:1–5)	*159*
39	It's Time to Go Home (2 Timothy 4:6–8)	*163*
40	God Appoints Our Disappointments (2 Timothy 4:10–22)	*167*

TITUS

41	Hope in a Hopeless World (Titus 1:1–4)	*173*
42	Authority Authors Hope (Titus 1:5–9)	*177*
43	Facing False Teachers (Titus 1:10–16)	*181*
44	Sound Doctrine and Sound Life (Titus 2:1–6)	*185*
45	A Good Show-Off (Titus 2:7–8)	*189*
46	"I Hate My Boss" (Titus 2:9–10)	*193*
47	Do You Have a Trainer? (Titus 2:11–14)	*197*
48	Can People Change? (Titus 3:1–7)	*201*
49	Profit and Loss (Titus 3:8–10)	*205*
50	Do Your Best (Titus 3:12–15)	*209*

Introduction to the StoryChanger Devotionals

Do you want to know the Bible's Story better, but don't know how? Do you want to change your story, but don't know how? Do you want to share the Bible's Story and the way it has changed your story, but don't know how? The StoryChanger Devotional series is the answer to this triple *how*.

How can I know the Bible better? At different points in my Christian life, I've tried to use various helps to go deeper in personal Bible study, but I found commentaries were too long and technical, whereas study Bibles were too brief and not practical.

How can I change my life for the better? I knew the Bible's Story was meant to change my story but couldn't figure out how to connect God's Story with my story in a transformative way. I was stuck, static, and frustrated at my lack of change, growth, and progress.

How can I share God's Story better? I've often been embarrassed by how slow and ineffective I am at sharing God's Story one-on-one. I know God's Story relates to other people's stories and that God's Story can change others' stories for the better, but I'm reluctant to seek out opportunities and hesitant when they arise.

So how about a series of books that teach us the Bible's Story in a way that helps to change our story and equips us to tell the Story to others. Or, to put it another way, how about books that teach us God's Story in a way that changes ours and others' stories?

After writing *The StoryChanger: How God Rewrites Our Story by Inviting Us into His* as an introduction to Jesus as the transformer of our stories, I thought, "Okay, what now? That's the theory, what about the practice? That's the introduction, but what about the next chapters? Jesus is the StoryChanger, but how can his Story change my story in practical ways on a daily basis? And how do I share his life-changing Story with others?"

I looked for daily devotionals that would take me through books of the Bible in a way that explained God's Story, changed my story, and equipped me to tell God's Story to others in a life-changing way. When I couldn't find any resources that had all three elements, I thought, "I'll write some devotionals for myself to help me know God's Story, change my story, and tell the story to others."

A few weeks later COVID hit, and I decided to start sharing these devotionals with the congregation I was serving at the time. I wanted to keep them connected with God and one another through that painful period of prolonged isolation from church and from one another.

I found that, like myself, people seemed to be hungry for daily devotionals that were more than emotional. They enjoyed daily devotionals that were educational, transformational, and missional. We worked our way verse-by-verse through books of the Bible with a focus on brevity, simplicity, clarity, practicality, and shareability. The StoryChanger started changing our stories with his Story, turning us into storytellers and therefore storychangers too.

Although these devotionals will take only about five minutes a day, I'm not promising you quick fixes. No, the StoryChanger usually changes our stories little by little. But over months and years of exposure to the StoryChanger's Story, he rewrites our story, and, through us, rewrites others' stories too.

To encourage you, I invite you to join the StoryChangers community at www.thestorychanger.life. There you can sign up for the weekly StoryChangers newsletter and subscribe to the StoryChangers podcast. Let's build a community of storychangers, committed Christians who dedicate themselves to knowing God's Story better, being changed by God's Story for the better, and sharing God's Story better. We'll meet the StoryChanger, have our stories changed, and become storychangers. I look forward to meeting you there and together changing stories with God's Story.[1]

---

[1] Some of this content originally appeared on *The Living the Bible podcast*, which has since been replaced by *The StoryChanger podcast,* https://podcasts.apple.com/us/podcast/the-storychanger/id1581826891.

Introduction to *Timothy and Titus: Stories of Fear and Courage*

The pastoral letters reveal how the apostle Paul used God's Story to strengthen and encourage two overwhelmed and fearful young pastors, Titus and Timothy. These young men were facing the daunting challenge of establishing and ordering new churches full of new Christians in pagan cultures.

Although the pastoral letters are addressed primarily to leaders in the church, they contain much spiritual instruction about how to relate to our spiritual leaders, how to support them, and how to benefit from them. Also, as always, Paul uses every opportunity to point us to Christ and the gospel, whatever our roles in the church or the culture might be.

May these stories of fear and courage change our stories and make us storytellers so that we become storychangers too.

1 TIMOTHY

If we don't fight
against anything,
we won't have
anything left
to fight for.

 Hear God's Story | Change Your Story | Tell the Story | Change Others' Stories

1

Fighting for Love

1 TIMOTHY 1:1–5

Some Christians are called to be courageous and others to be compassionate, right?

Wrong. Although many think that being courageous means you cannot be compassionate (and vice versa), the apostle Paul unites these two virtues in 1 Timothy 1:1–5 when he calls Timothy and us to unite them in our lives. *How do we unite courage and compassion?*

Timothy had a problem with timidity, prompting Paul to write this letter to *en*courage him—to put courage in him—and to also advance the cause of love. Let's use this letter to Timothy to grow in both compassion and courage.

We Must Fight Falsehood 1:1–4

Paul briefly greets Timothy (1:1–2), before launching into a vigorous call to arms: "As I urged you when I was going to Macedonia, remain at Ephesus so that you may charge certain persons not to teach any different doctrine, nor to devote themselves to myths and endless genealogies, which promote speculations" (1:3–4).

Paul harnesses a military word—*charge*—to convey the idea of forceful authority. He demands Timothy fight on two fronts. He is to oppose "any different doctrine" (1:3), meaning novel teaching of any kind, and divisive ideas, which he calls "myths and endless genealogies, which promote speculations" (1:4).

If we don't fight against anything,
we won't have anything left to fight for.

"If we are to fight against human disorder, what do we fight for?"
We fight for God's order.

We Must Fight for God's Order 1:4

In contrast to the novel teaching and divisive speculations of the false teachers, Timothy is to devote himself to "the stewardship from God that is by faith" (1:4). *Stewardship* means "order," and here it's an order that comes "from God," in contrast to the chaos that came from false teachers. Such divine order "is by faith," meaning it results from believing God's truth.

Fighting usually produces chaos,
but this fighting produces order.

"That sounds like a lot of fighting.
Isn't Christianity all about love?"
Yes, it's love we're fighting for.

We Must Fight for Love 1:5

Paul commands Timothy to fight *against* chaotic falsehood and *for* God's order, but he insists that "the aim of our charge is love" (1:5). Despite the common tendency to separate courage from compassion, biblical courage is not against compassion but actually assists it. The two are not in contrast but complement each other.

So, we have the charge and we have the end goal. What's the plan? How do we get from the charge to the goal, from fighting to love? Paul lays out a three-step plan. This love "issues from a pure heart and a good conscience and a sincere faith" (1:5). The purer our hearts, the clearer our consciences, and the more genuine our faith, the faster and closer we get to the great goal of love and compassion.

Fight because you love,
and you'll love because you fought.

Changing Our Story with God's Story

At various points in my life, I've lacked courage. Other times I've lacked compassion. Many times I've been courageous when compassion was more appropriate, and compassionate when courage was more needed. Where then do we turn when we fail, fail, and fail again?

We turn to Christ who is the greatest fighter and the greatest lover. He fights because he loves and loves because he fights. He fights against falsehood, he fights for God's order, and he fights for love. He has a perfectly pure heart, a perfectly good conscience, and a perfectly sincere faith. He therefore has perfect love. We stand in awe at his impeccable compassion, his impeccable courage, and his impeccable combination of them. His perfect combination of courage and compassion covers our imperfect courage, our imperfect compassion, and our imperfect combination of them.

Summary: How can we unite courage and compassion? *Fight against falsehood and for God's order to maximize Christ-like love.*

Question: In what area of life is God calling you to show courageous compassion?

Prayer: Compassionate and courageous Savior, help me to follow your three-step plan to compassionate courage.

If we get the law wrong, we'll get the gospel wrong.

 Hear God's Story | Change Your Story | Tell the Story | Change Others' Stories

2

Theological Terrorists

1 TIMOTHY 1:6-11

After 9/11, we were shocked at the pictures that showed the terrorists going through airport security. They didn't look like jihadis. We were surprised because they looked like everyday businessmen or leisure travelers. They looked normal and harmless, and yet their hearts were full of despicable evil. No scanner or pat-down could have detected the malice behind their mundaneness. They appeared to pose no threat to anyone, so no one was alerted or alarmed to take action against them.

In 1 Timothy 1:6-11, the apostle Paul provides a heart scanner to reveal the danger of false teachers, so that Timothy will take decisive action against them to protect the gospel and the church. *What does God's scanner reveal about theological terrorists?*

Theological Terrorists Have Hateful Hearts 1:6a

When the devil sends false teachers into the church of Christ, they rarely look like theological terrorists. The devil doesn't identify his agents with a sign around their necks saying, "I am a false teacher and a deadly threat to you all." No, usually false teachers are highly plausible. They use the Bible and quote the Bible. They are often educated, talented, and superconfident in their persuasive words. Thankfully, God's scanner helps us see into their hearts so that we will protect the gospel and God's people from them.

God's heart-scanner reveals that while the godly are characterized by "love that issues from a pure heart and a good conscience and a sincere faith," the false teachers, "by swerving from these, have wandered away" (1:5–6). In contrast to the godly, whose hearts are filled with love, false teachers wander away from love and into hate.

False teaching begins with a false heart.

"Why do false teachers do this?"
They are interested only in themselves.

Theological Terrorists Have Selfish Aims 1:6–7

Where does their wandering take them? They "have wandered away into vain discussion, desiring to be teachers of the law, without understanding either what they are saying or the things about which they make confident assertions" (1:6–7).

They multiply impressive words, which result in minimal value, they want teaching positions of prestige and power, and they are confident but clueless. Their hate-filled hearts have selfish aims.

Our words inflate our egos, but God's word deflates our egos.

"What's their main tactic?"
They misuse the Bible.

Theological Terrorists Abuse the Bible 1:8–11

God's good law can have good effects if it is used in a good way. "Now we know that the law is good, if one uses it lawfully" (1:8). What's a good use of the law? When it convicts us of sin and reveals gospel need (1:9–10). It's certainly not for academic speculation and showing off. We aren't to use God's law to write a story of self-salvation, self-confidence, or self-glory. It writes a story of God-salvation, God-confidence, and God-glory.

The Bible is to convict of sin, not create sin.

"What's the effect of all this?"
Spiritual genocide.

Theological Terrorists Destroy Needy Souls 1:9–11

Paul says his good use of the law is "in accordance with the gospel of the glory of the blessed God with which I have been entrusted" (1:11). If the law is not used as God intended, then sinners are not convicted of their sin, and therefore do not hear or want the glorious gospel. The result is lost souls, lost heaven, and a lost eternity.

If we get the law wrong, we'll get the gospel wrong.

> ### Changing Our Story with God's Story
>
> Christ alone can protect us from false hearts, hateful hearts, selfish hearts, and rebellious hearts in ourselves and others. May he give us loving, serving, caring gospel hearts so that our story never includes a chapter called "Taken by Surprise Terrorist Attack."
>
> **Summary:** What does God's scanner reveal about theological terrorists? *Overcome timidity by treating false teachers as theological terrorists who abuse the Bible and destroy souls.*
>
> **Question:** What theological terrorists threaten you, your family, or your church?
>
> **Prayer:** Blessed God, help me to defend the gospel you've entrusted to me from those who use it for their own gain at the expense of others.

Natural gifts that we abuse can be turned to spiritual gifts God can use.

 Hear God's Story | Change Your Story | Tell the Story | Change Others' Stories

3

Christ Trusts the Untrustworthy with His Trustworthy Gospel

1 TIMOTHY 1:11–12

Imagine if it were your job to carry around the president's briefcase containing the codes to launch nuclear missiles, known as the "nuclear football." It would be an incredibly intimidating, awesome, worrying job, wouldn't it? But if you were chosen by the president, equipped by the president, trained by the president, and had the full confidence of the president, that would transform your perspective and even make you thankful for such a trust and privilege.

In 1 Timothy 1:11–12, the apostle Paul speaks of something awesome being given to him and Timothy—not the destructive power of launching a nuclear weapon that can blow the world to pieces, but the constructive power of the gospel that can put this broken world back together again. Even though it is a constructive power, it is still a massive responsibility. No wonder Timothy was intimidated. We are too, at times, and ask ourselves, *How can I bear the weight of gospel responsibility?* Paul encourages Timothy and us by using himself as an example.

Christ Entrusts Us with Gospel Service 1:11

Christ has given us a massive message with massive trust. As Paul says, it's "the gospel of the glory of the blessed God with which I have been entrusted" (1:11). It doesn't get bigger than that. What an awesome responsibility. What an awesome trust Christ placed in us when he gave us the glorious gospel.

Christ trusts the untrustworthy with his trustworthy gospel.

"How can I carry this massive trust?"
Only in Christ's strength.

Christ Strengthens Us for Gospel Service 1:12

We can carry this massive trust because of Christ's massive strengthening, which leads to massive thanksgiving. As Paul says, "I thank him who has given me strength, Christ Jesus our Lord" (1:12).

The best way to experience Christ's strength
is to experience our own weakness.

"But will I keep going to the end?" Christ sustains and keeps
us in the beginning, the middle, and the end.

Christ Keeps Us in Gospel Service 1:12

When Paul writes that "[Christ] judged me faithful" (1:12), he doesn't mean that God saved or called Paul because of his past or future faithfulness. No, the whole context emphasizes Paul's gratitude for God's sovereign and merciful intervention in his life.

Rather, Paul is explaining how redirected natural gifts can become spiritual gifts. Christ saw Paul's natural single-mindedness and determination and knew he could redirect and refine them for the sake of the gospel. Paul's fiery, intense zeal that had been dedicated to the destruction of the church would now be used in the service of the church. "He judged me faithful" is about what Christ would make him become by his grace. Christ entrusted him with the gospel, and Christ made him trustworthy.

Natural gifts that we abuse can be turned to spiritual gifts God can use.

"But what if I or others doubt my calling?"
Remember Christ's calling.

Christ Appoints Us to Gospel Service 1:12

When Paul himself or anyone else doubted his responsibility or abilities, he would point to Christ's "appointing me to his service" (1:12). When people point to our disappointments, let's point ourselves to God's appointment.

Christ's appointment helps us persevere through disappointments.

Changing Our Story with God's Story

Like Paul, I was a determined strong-willed young man in my non-Christian years. Sadly, it was a destructive strength—until Christ intervened. Jesus changed my story by taking my natural single-mindedness that was destroying me (and others) and turning it into a spiritual single-mindedness that would reconstruct me and eventually others too. God continues to use this passage to encourage me with Christ's trust, Christ's strength, Christ's preservation, and Christ's appointment, especially when I'm feeling timid. We need weighty grace to carry weighty grace.

Summary: How can I bear the weight of gospel responsibility? *When feeling timid about serving Christ, use Christ's trust, Christ's strengthening, Christ's keeping, and Christ's appointment to encourage yourself.*

Question: If you feel untrustworthy to carry the gospel, how can you use the gospel to help you carry the gospel?

Prayer: Trustworthy Savior, strengthen me with the gospel to carry the gospel.

God can use our great sin to motivate great service.

 Hear God's Story | Change Your Story | Tell the Story | Change Others' Stories

4

Great Sin, Great Salvation, and Great Service

1 TIMOTHY 1:13–17

"I've sinned too much to be saved." "I've sinned too much to serve." Ever had these fears? I have, and sometimes still do. The first fear, "I've sinned too much to be saved," makes me feel hopeless. The second fear, "I've sinned too much to serve," makes me feel useless. Hopeless and useless are paralyzing feelings. *How can we get to hopeful and useful when we feel hopeless and useless?* In 1 Timothy 1:13–17, Paul encourages Timothy that great sin is no barrier to salvation or service.

Great Sin Is No Barrier to Salvation 1:13–14

Paul had overflowing sin: "Formerly I was a blasphemer, persecutor, and insolent opponent" (1:13). In the previous verses, Paul wrote about what God had made him by grace, but he never forgot what he once was by nature. His sinful past further magnified God's grace in putting him into the ministry.

Paul got overflowing grace. "But I received mercy because I had acted ignorantly in unbelief" (1:13). The biblical principle behind this statement is "less knowledge results in less responsibility." In contrast to the false teachers who knew Christian truth and had made a Christian profession of faith, Paul did not know the gospel and had not professed faith when he committed egregious sins.

"And the grace of our Lord overflowed for me with the faith and love that are in Christ Jesus (1:14). This is what it took to save Paul—superabundant grace, exceedingly abundant grace, torrential grace, overflowing grace. That drenching grace of Christ brought with it two bonuses: faith in Christ and love for Christ.

God drowns us in grace to save us from drowning in guilt.

"It's wonderful that my great sin is no barrier to salvation, but is it a barrier to serving Christ?"
Both barriers are zero centimeters high.

Great Sin Is No Barrier to Service 1:15–16

"The saying is trustworthy and deserving of full acceptance" (1:15). A "saying" was a catchphrase, a soundbite, a short pithy saying that helped people remember important teachings. But this saying is more than Tweet-worthy; it's "trustworthy" and therefore "deserving of full acceptance" with full confidence.

So, what is the saying? "Christ Jesus came into the world to save sinners, of whom I am the foremost" (1:15). He didn't come just to set an example, or just to show he cared, or just to help sinners; he came to justify sinners. That he came into the world is amazing; to save, even more amazing; to save sinners is past amazing; to save the greatest of all sinners, is mind-blowing.

Why would anyone want to save Paul, the chief of all sinners? Paul asked that too but got this answer: "I received mercy for this reason, that in me, as the foremost, Jesus Christ might display his perfect patience as an example to those who were to believe in him for eternal life" (1:16). Paul was a pattern, a specimen, a prototype, an exhibit of who God saves, how God saves, and why God saves. The ultimate sinner became a saint. The chief sinner became the chief apostle.

God can use our great sin to motivate great service.

Changing Our Story with God's Story

Not only is great sin no barrier to salvation or service, but God also uses great sinners to show his great salvation and to do great service. It's no wonder that this story of great salvation and great service leads Paul and us to great praise: "To the King of the ages, immortal, invisible, the only God, be honor and glory forever and ever. Amen" (1:17). Give God great praise for his great salvation and great service despite our great sin.

Summary: How can we get hope and be useful? *Banish hopelessness and uselessness by asking God to use great sinners to show his great salvation and do great service.*

Question: What great sin is keeping you back from salvation or service?

Prayer: Great Savior, I am a great sinner. Therefore, save me and use me in your service.

Church discipline is to rescue the shipwrecked, not to sink their ships.

 Hear God's Story | Change Your Story | Tell the Story | Change Others' Stories

5

Delivered to Satan

1 TIMOTHY 1:18–20

Afghanistan 2015, and the United State's war against the Taliban was in its fourteenth year. A reporter interviewed a small company of American soldiers on a mountaintop outpost that was under daily attack from unseen Taliban snipers and random rocket fire. Regularly losing their buddies, these soldiers were completely demoralized. Although they halfheartedly fired back at times, they had no hope of accomplishing anything.

I've thought about this painful TV report many times because it's easy for Christians to get into the same defeatist mindset, especially when we're in a long war and taking casualties. *How do we maintain a fighting spirit through many chapters of loss?* In 1 Timothy 1:18–20, Paul encourages Timothy to maintain a fighting spirit when he was losing heart for the battle.

We Have a Good Commission 1:18

"This charge I entrust to you, Timothy, my child, in accordance with the prophecies previously made about you" (1:18). This charge is the responsibility Paul laid upon Timothy in verse 3, to confront the false teachers. Paul reminds Timothy of this charge because a divine call to ministry confirmed by God's people is a powerful motivator and encourager in difficult times.

If we forget our call to fight, we'll forget to fight when we're called.

"So is the cause worth it?"
Yes, it's the best possible cause.

We Have a Good Cause 1:18

What's the effect of God's call and the church's confirmation? "By them you may wage the good warfare" (1:18). Timothy, this is worth fighting for, worth suffering for. You cannot remain neutral. You've got to get into this fight and go all in. War is war; it's all or nothing, do or die, life or death. The eternal destiny of souls and the glory of God rests on the outcome.

Fight with all your worth because this is a cause worth fighting for.

"Do I have any weapons for the battle?"
Here are a few.

We Have Good Weapons 1:19–20

With one hand we are "holding faith" (1:19), clinging to the truth of the gospel and believing in the gospel in the midst of war. With the other hand we're holding "a good conscience" (1:19), which guides us through the storm like the rudder on a boat. Ignoring your conscience in the storm is like throwing your rudder overboard. A good Christian must be a good soldier and a good sailor.

"By rejecting this [a good conscience] some have made shipwreck of their faith" (1:19). They discarded their rudder, hit the rocks, and now their lives and cargo are strewn across the water. Two of these rudderless believers were "Hymenaeus and Alexander, whom I have handed over to Satan that they may learn not to blaspheme" (1:20). This final step in church discipline says to an erring church member, "We love you, but we do not view you as a member of God's family. You are now exposed to Satan without the protections and privileges of God's family."

Although this sounds harsh, the ultimate aim is not damnation but reclamation, "that they may learn not to blaspheme" (1:20). Faith, a good conscience, and church discipline are good weapons.

Church discipline is to rescue the shipwrecked, not to sink their ships.

Changing Our Story with God's Story

We will lose heart for the battle if we forget our orders, if we forget what we're fighting for, if we forget our weapons, or if we forget the aim of the salvation of sinners. We have a good commission, good weapons, and a great cause. Above all we have a great captain of our salvation who goes before us into battle and fights not only with us but for us.

Summary: How do we maintain a fighting spirit through many chapters of loss? *Remember God's good call and use good weapons to wage a good war with a good aim for our good captain, for a good story with a good ending.*

Question: What discourages you in the battle, and how will you use Paul's charge to encourage you?

Prayer: Captain of Our Salvation, revive my spirit to fight with all my might.

Prayer is not a checklist. It's a heartcheck.

Hear God's Story | Change Your Story | Tell the Story | Change Others' Stories

6

The Prayer Pivot

1 TIMOTHY 2:1-3

Pastor and author F. B. Meyer was rooming with A. B. Simpson (founder of the Christian and Missionary Alliance) at a missionary conference. One morning Meyer woke up to discover Simpson weeping in prayer as he clutched a globe of the world. Prayer turned him to God and prayer turned him to people.

Timid Timothy, on the other hand, was more fearful when it came to ministry and outreach in a hostile world. Like me, you've probably felt more like Timothy than A. B. Simpson. *How then do we turn from self to God and from self to people?* In 1 Timothy 2:1–2, Paul uses prayer to pivot Timothy from self to God and from self to people.

Prayer Pivots Our Hearts to God 2:1

"First of all, then, I urge that supplications, prayers, intercessions, and thanksgivings be made" (2:1). The first step for Timothy is prayer. Paul is effectively saying, "Timothy, turn your heart from self to God, and he will turn your heart to people. He'll give you a big heart, a fearless heart, and a loving heart."

There are small but significant differences between the different words for prayer in verse 1. *Supplications* arise from a sense of need and are specific requests for specific needs. *Prayers* is a catchall word for prayer, but with an emphasis on bringing requests to God in a worshipful spirit. *Intercessions* are bold pleas on behalf of others and involve advocacy and empathy. *Thanksgivings* remind us that prayer is not just about getting things from God but also about giving to God.

Paul's not saying, "Check off these different kinds of prayer," but, "Pray lots of prayers." Prayer is not about working through a checklist but pouring out our hearts to God.

Prayer is not a checklist. It's a heartcheck.

"What happens when we pivot to God in prayer?"
God pivots our hearts to people.

Prayer Pivots Our Hearts to People 2:2

These multiple prayers are to be "for all people, for kings and all who are in high positions, that we may lead a peaceful and quiet life, godly and dignified in every way" (2:1–2). When we pour out our hearts to God, God pours out his heart in us, so that we pour out our hearts for others.

We are to pray all kinds of prayer for all kinds of people and specific prayers for specific people. The specific people are world leaders, and the specific prayer is for "peace and quiet." Although the church was facing increasing persecution, Paul's solution was not to run away from these leaders but to run to God in prayer for them. He asked God for "peace and quiet" because these are the best conditions for practicing, commending, and spreading the gospel. He wasn't asking the state to support the church but just to leave her alone so that Christians could live a godly and dignified life.

When we pivot out our hearts to God,
God pivots our hearts toward people.

Changing Our Story with God's Story

Do you need more encouragement to pray such prayers for such people with such a purpose? Listen to verse 3: "This is good, and it is pleasing in the sight of God our Savior" (2:3). God loves to hear these prayers because he loves the God-like hearts behind them. Such prayers take us deep into the heart of our Savior, making our hearts like his. Turn your heart to the Lord, and he'll turn your heart to people. Bring your small, scared, and self-centered heart to your Savior, and he will give you his heart for people: big, courageous, and loving.

Summary: How do we turn from self to God and from self to people? *Use prayer to turn your heart to God, and he'll turn your heart to people.*

Question: How will Timothy's prayer story change your prayer story?

Prayer: Our God and Savior, share your big heart for this big world with me so that I can pray big prayers for big numbers of people and so share in your big purpose for the world.

"All people" prayer is to be offered to an "all people" Savior.

 Hear God's Story | Change Your Story | Tell the Story | Change Others' Stories

7

Our "All People" Savior

1 TIMOTHY 2:3-4

If we're honest, sometimes we do not equally desire the salvation of all kinds of people. We must confess that while there are some kinds of people we really want to be saved, there are other kinds of people for whom our desire for their salvation is weak or even nonexistent. That's a problem, because it's contrary to God's character and God's heart. *How can we expand our narrow hearts to desire the salvation of all people?* In 1 Timothy 2:1–4, Paul encourages Timothy and the people he pastors to expand their hearts to include all people in their prayers and evangelism.

We Pray to an "All People" Savior 2:3-4

The first two verses of 1 Timothy 2 instruct us to pray "all people" prayers. Why? Because we pray to an "all people" Savior. "This [kind of prayer] is good, and it is pleasing in the sight of God our Savior" (2:3). Why should God's people pray so globally? Because God's salvation is so global.

He is God our Savior, but he wants to be more than *our* Savior. God "desires all people to be saved and to come to the knowledge of the truth" (2:4). Does this mean God will save everyone? Does it mean he wants to save everyone but evidently fails? Or does it mean something else?

The wider context is key to understanding this specific text. Remember, in chapter 1, Paul urged Timothy to fight against false

Jewish teachers. These were elitists, people who specialized in complicated, speculative interpretations of Old Testament genealogies. They regarded themselves as a higher spiritual class. They prided themselves on secret insight and special knowledge that few others had. They spent all their days in idle and pointless debate. In other words, they were an exclusive club that few were invited to join.

Paul is contrasting this inward-looking, introverted, narrow mindset with God's global heart and worldview. He is contrasting their "few people" approach with God's "all people" (meaning, "all kinds of people") approach.

"All people" prayer is to be offered to an "all people" Savior.

"What's the impact of such 'all people' prayers?"
They change others and they also change us.

We're to Be an "All People" People 2:3–4

This passage is partly about the heart and will of God, but it's mainly about the heart and will of God's people. It deals a hammer blow to racism, nationalism, denominationalism, classism, parochialism, and so on.

If all people matter to God, then all people must be given the truth so that they can be saved and come to a knowledge of the truth. Don't hold back your prayers from anyone, don't hold back your heart from anyone, don't hold back the truth from anyone.

Pray "all people" prayers with "all people" hearts
as you witness with an "all people" gospel.

Changing Our Story with God's Story

Jesus has the widest heart in the world. His massive heart shatters the man-made barriers of prejudice, bigotry, chauvinism, racism, nationalism, elitism, and every other kind of sinful *-ism*.

The Christian life begins with Christ's heart being transplanted into ours, and that life continues by Christ's heart expanding wider and wider in our lives. At best our hearts become shriveled raisins compared with his ripe-to-burst watermelon, but one day, in a moment, our dry little raisins will become like a perfect watermelon.

Summary: How do we expand our narrow hearts? *Worship the "all people" Savior to become an "all people" person.*

Question: What people will notice the impact of this verse on your heart, your prayers, and your witness?

Prayer: All Kinds of People Savior, give me an all kinds of people heart, all kinds of people prayers, and an all kinds of people witness.

God required a ransom, paid the ransom, and became the ransom.

 Hear God's Story | Change Your Story | Tell the Story | Change Others' Stories

8

The Limits of an Unlimited Salvation

1 TIMOTHY 2:5-7

The majority of unbelievers believe that everyone is going to heaven no matter what religion they follow or even if they follow no religion at all. Unbelievers believe in an unlimited salvation.

The majority of believers rightly say that salvation is limited to those who put their trust in Christ. However, they often limit who hears that message. They may not say it out loud, but effectively they are saying, "There's no point in telling certain kinds of people about the only way of salvation." Believers sometimes believe in a limited audience for salvation.

What's the Bible's answer to unbelievers' unlimited salvation and believers' limited audience for salvation? In 1 Timothy 2:5–7, the apostle Paul teaches both a limited salvation and an unlimited audience.

Salvation Is Limited in Its Means 2:5-6

The "means" is the way something is accomplished. For example, a pipe is the means or the vehicle of transferring water from a reservoir to our faucets.

So, what is the means of salvation? What's the vehicle for getting saved? There's only one way, one vehicle, and that's Christ, whom Paul describes in two ways.

Christ is the only mediator. "For there is one God, and there is one mediator between God and men, the man Christ Jesus" (2:5). A mediator is an intermediary, a person in the middle who reconciles two rival parties by resolving the reason for their dispute and alienation.

- *Jesus is a necessary mediator.* There's an infinite gulf between us and a holy God, and therefore we need someone to bridge the gap.
- *Jesus is a two-sided mediator.* There are problems on both sides. God has a problem with us, and we have a problem with God.
- *Jesus is a qualified mediator.* He's qualified by his relation to both parties: he is both God and man.
- *Jesus is the only mediator.* That's the primary focus here. There is no other way to be saved. No other vehicle, no other channel, no other means of salvation.

Christ goes between us and God, to bridge the gap between us and God.

Christ is the only ransom. "Christ Jesus, who gave himself as a ransom for all, which is the testimony given at the proper time" (2:5–6). A ransom is a payment that purchases someone's release from bondage, captivity, or slavery. In this case, the payer becomes the payment. It's a substitute ransom for those who could not pay it or be it. It's his blood instead of our blood.

*God required a ransom, paid the ransom,
and became the ransom.*

*"Does this limited salvation limit our message?"
Quite the opposite.*

Salvation Is Unlimited in Its Message 2:7

"For this I was appointed a preacher and an apostle (I am telling the truth, I am not lying), a teacher of the Gentiles in faith and truth"

(2:7). If there were many gods and many ways of salvation, there would be no need for a global offer of the gospel. The global offer of salvation through Christ is necessary because there is only one God, and Christ is the only mediator and the only ransom.

An exclusive faith (there is one God and one salvation) means an inclusive mission (all must hear). That's why God appointed Paul as an apostle to the Gentiles. The gospel had to be communicated beyond its Jewish beginnings to the whole world. The uniqueness of Christ requires the universality of the gospel.

The limited way of salvation demands an unlimited offer of salvation.

> ### Changing Our Story with God's Story
>
> In saying that Christ's salvation is limited, we are not diminishing its power, but rather emphasizing that salvation is only for those who put their faith in Christ. It's a limitation that funnels people into the only salvation powerful enough to save.
>
> **Summary:** What's the Bible's answer to unbelievers' unlimited salvation and believers' limited audience for salvation? *Get clarity about the limited means of salvation, to be more convinced and clear in your unlimited message of salvation.*
>
> **Question:** What salvation error do you fall into, and how will you correct it?
>
> **Prayer:** Great Savior, use me as a means of bringing your limited salvation to an unlimited number of people.

You can't be poisonous in private relationships and pious in public prayer.

 Hear God's Story | Change Your Story | Tell the Story | Change Others' Stories

9

Male Sins

1 TIMOTHY 2:8

Are there gender-specific sins? Or, to put it another way, are there sins that men are particularly susceptible to? If so, are there sins that women are especially susceptible to?

In 1 Timothy 2:8–15, the apostle Paul identifies two sexes, male and female, distinguishes between them, and then addresses sins that each are prone to, and that can be especially problematic in the church. First, *what are common male sins in the church?* Paul addresses two in verse 8:

- *Men can be too passive*, too scared to lead
- *Men can be too aggressive*, too angry to pray

Paul began discussing public worship in 2:1–2. Having digressed in verses 3–7 to speak of the great salvation and the great Savior that motivates our worship and prayer, he returns to the details of public worship in verse 8 and following.

Men Are to Lead in Public Prayer 2:8

"I desire then that in every place the men should pray" (2:8). When Paul says "I desire," he's not just expressing a personal preference. The word behind *desire* means "based upon reason" and is often used to describe an authoritative command. He is therefore commanding and demanding that men pray.

But where are they to pray? "In every place" can mean everywhere or in every place the church gathers (1 Cor. 1:2). As this is a pastoral epistle addressing church life, it most likely is referring to the official assembly of the church for public worship.

And who is to pray? "The men should pray." The Greek word here for "men" is the specific word for male as opposed to female. It doesn't necessarily exclude women, but it definitely includes men. When it comes to public prayer in church, men must step up to the plate, take responsibility, and lead the congregation in prayer. Passivity is not an option.

Passive leaders are poor leaders.

"If that's the who and where of prayer, what's the how of prayer?"
Pray with faith-full hands and love-full hearts.

Men Are to Pray with Holy Hands and Hearts 2:8

Having instructed Timothy in who should pray and where they should pray, Paul then turns to the *how* of prayer, addressing both the physical posture and spiritual manner: ". . . men should pray, lifting holy hands without anger or quarreling" (2:8).

"Lifting holy hands" is a physical posture that says, "We are weak, and we extend our hands to the one who can help us." Not only does lifting hands outwardly express an inner dependence on God, but the physical action may also help deepen that dependence.

Having encouraged a dependent relationship on God in prayer, Paul then calls for a loving relationship with others. They are to pray "without anger or quarreling." The problem in Ephesus was that instead of men praying with clean hands, they prayed with clenched fists!

I once interned at a church in Scotland. The weekly prayer meeting was like a war zone as two of the men engaged in theological battle in their public prayers. Such angry and argumentative spirits were not conducive to prayer.

You can't be poisonous in private relationships
and pious in public prayer.

Changing Our Story with God's Story

Men can be too passive or too aggressive. To the passive, the apostle Paul says, "Men are to lead in public worship." To the aggressive, Paul says, "Men are to lead with holy hands and hearts."

Although we are discouraged by how sin can enter the most holy actions, like prayer, we are brought to worship when we consider how Jesus modeled this perfectly. Never erring in either passivity or aggression, he prayed at the right time, in the right places, and in the right way. And his prayer-righteousness is given to us when we believe in him.

Summary: What are common male sins in the church? *Replace fear-full passivity with faith-full activity, and angry aggression with loving affection, if you want public worship to be heavenly worship.*

Question: What steps can you take to avoid the errors of being too passive or too aggressive?

Prayer: Perfect Prayer, thank you for praying perfectly for me. Teach me how to pray as you prayed.

If appearance
is your focus,
God will be
out of focus.

 Hear God's Story | Change Your Story | Tell the Story | Change Others' Stories

10

What Is a Beautiful Woman?

1 TIMOTHY 2:9–10

What is a beautiful woman? The world's answer to that question changes every year. So if our primary question is, "How can I be beautiful?" we'll never have the right answer for long. Not only is the world constantly changing, but we as individuals change as we age. *How can I be beautiful and stay beautiful?*

In the last devotional, we looked at an especially male sin—being too angry to pray. In 1 Timothy 2:9–10, Paul identifies a particularly female sin—being too pretty to work. He wanted the Christian women in Ephesus to shift their focus from impressive appearance to practical Christianity.

Don't Focus on Elaborate Hair or Extravagant Clothes 2:9

"Likewise also that women should adorn themselves . . . not with braided hair and gold or pearls or costly attire" (2:9). If you went into the Ephesian church and looked out across the congregation, you would see row after row of braided and bejeweled hair. The pews were filled with fancy hairstyles topped off with numerous precious stones.

To accompany their elaborate hairstyles, the women wore "costly attire." They were dressing for church in the latest high and extravagant fashions. There's nothing wrong and plenty right about nice clothes (Prov. 31:22) and attractive jewelry (Song 1:10–11; Isa.

61:10). The problem in the Ephesian church was excessive—and even exclusive—concern about what they wore. They went to church not to be worshipers but to be worshiped.

If appearance is your focus,
God will be out of focus.

"So, what should I wear? Should I never try to be pretty?"
Let Christ give you a new wardrobe.

Focus on Fitting Modesty and Beautiful Practicality 2:9–10

"Likewise also that women should adorn themselves in respectable apparel, with modesty and self-control . . . with what is proper for women who profess godliness—with good works" (2:9–10).

"Respectable apparel" means clothes that are becoming, appropriate, and suitable for a Christian woman. "With modesty" means keeping within the bounds of what is decent and proper. "With self-control" means not dressing seductively or suggestively, and not overspending on clothes. To put it bluntly, as a child of God you shouldn't dress like a prostitute.

Having emptied their wardrobes of what is not becoming, Paul then fills them up with what is most becoming and beautifying for a godly woman—good works. The Bible commends four areas of good works specific to women: devoted service to their husbands and children, hospitality to Christians and non-Christians, mentoring of younger women, and care for the poor (1 Tim. 5:10–15; Titus 2:3–5). These kinds of good works make women beautiful and attractive to God and to others.

What is a beautiful woman? Here's God's answer. Do something beautiful for God, and you'll become beautiful doing it. Good works reveal and even reform a good heart. That kind of beauty can grow with age, stopping and even reversing the aging process.

Paul contrasts the artificial glamor of the world with the true beauty of a godly life; the cheapness of expensive clothes with the value of godly character and service. The most beautiful people in the church are those clothed with good works.

True beauty isn't skin-deep; it's soul-deep.

Changing Our Story with God's Story

In the last devotional, we heard Paul exhort the men to speak godly *words*. In this devotional, Paul exhorts the women to do godly *works*. When we focus on self, we live for people to say, "You're so beautiful!" When we focus on others, God says, "You're so beautiful."

Summary: How can I be beautiful and stay beautiful? *Do good works in faith for the best beauty therapy.*

Question: What good works will beautify you today?

Prayer: Beautiful God of Great Works, make me and all Christian women everywhere beautiful with good works.

Male and female roles are based on timeless truth not cultural considerations.

 Hear God's Story | Change Your Story | Tell the Story | Change Others' Stories

11

A Revolutionary Role for Women

1 TIMOTHY 2:11–15

God has a positive, broad, and constructive vision of a woman's role in this world, which, if followed, leads to female flourishing. Many in the world, though, are revolting against God's perfect plan for women and leading a mutiny against God's order, damaging many women and making the world a worse place.

In 1 Timothy 2:11–15, Paul invites us to join another kind of revolution, one that will turn the world upside down, but will have the effect of putting it the right way up. It's a constructive takeover that will make the world a better place. *How can we join the gospel revolution and change the world's story?* Paul begins with the specific roles God has designed for women.

The Christian Woman's Role Is Clear 2:11–12

The Bible teaches that men and women are essentially and spiritually equal, but physically and functionally different. Assuming that essential and spiritual equality, Paul outlines a woman's role in the church.

In a culture that viewed women as intellectually inferior to men and that educated only men, the words "Let a woman learn" (2:11) were liberating and dignifying. But while learning for women is in, certain kinds of teaching are out. "Let a woman learn quietly with all submissiveness. I do not permit a woman to teach or to exercise authority over a man; rather, she is to remain quiet" (2:11–12).

Men have much to learn from women, but there's one forum where that is not to take place, and that's the authoritative proclamation of God's word in public worship.

Knowing that this would be hard for many to accept, Paul called for "all submissiveness," which is a yielding to God-ordained authority. To submit to divine authority is to please and honor the Lord by cooperating with the way God has designed and ordered society.

Teaching and ruling may please us,
but learning and submitting please God.

"Why did God design the woman's role like this?"
There are two reasons.

The Christian Woman's Role Is Reasonable 2:13–14

The first reason Paul gives for God limiting the women's role is *the order of creation*. "Adam was formed first, then Eve" (2:13). In the Bible, being firstborn was not about superiority, but about authority and responsibility. When God made Adam first, he was not only creating our first parents; he was also establishing male-female roles and relationships for all time. God wants the creation order to be reflected in church order.

Paul then adds a second reason: *the order of sin*. "Adam was not deceived, but the woman was deceived and became a transgressor" (2:14). Look what happened when the creation order was reversed, when Adam gave up his God-given role and Eve took over a role that was not hers: disaster ensued.

Male and female roles are based on timeless truth
not cultural considerations.

"It's hard for many women to hear this."
Look at the encouragement God gives.

The Woman's Role Is Blessed 2:15

"Yet she will be saved through childbearing" (2:15). "Childbearing" is shorthand for having, protecting, and providing for children. If we follow God's order, we will not only be much happier; we will be much more influential as well. Women will exert godly influence from the bottom up, by Christlike influencing of children. Women can re-create world order by reinstating the creation order. This re-creation can only happen, though, "if they continue in faith and love and holiness, with self-control" (2:15). That's shorthand for following God's order.

Revert to God's order, and you'll revolutionize world order.

Changing Our Story with God's Story

When we see the (im)moral revolution destroying so many lives, we may be tempted to withdraw and hide. Instead, God calls godly women to the front line, to become child-raising revolutionaries that will save the world from destruction. Think of Mary, Jesus's mother, and how her submission to God's order changed the world order. Her revolutionary spirit lives on in godly women everywhere.

Summary: How can we join the gospel revolution and change the world's story? *Accept your God-appointed role and responsibilities, and you will massively influence children's stories, and therefore the church and the world, for good.*

Question: How can you advance God's revolution?

Prayer: Revolutionary God, begin your revolution in me, so that I can restore your perfect creation order.

The devil targets leaders because he knows leaders are targeting him.

Hear God's Story | Change Your Story | Tell the Story | Change Others' Stories

12

Christlike Leadership

1 TIMOTHY 3:1–7

How does your church pick its leaders? Here's what I've seen in many churches:

- Some churches pick older leaders who don't have the ability for the work.
- Some churches pick unqualified leaders who don't have the character for the work.
- Some churches pick young leaders who don't have the spiritual maturity for the work.

In 1 Timothy 3:1–7, God describes the Christlike leadership he wants to see in the church.

In the previous chapter the apostle Paul organized worship in the church. In this chapter, he moves on to leadership in the church. *What is Christlike leadership?*

Christlike Leadership Is a Good Aspiration 3:1

We know church leadership is important to God because this passage begins with the words, "The saying is trustworthy" (3:1). All the other "faithful sayings" of Paul are about salvation and sanctification.[1] By adding leadership to the trustworthy sayings, Paul is warning us that if we

---

1 1 Tim. 1:12–17; 4:8–10; 2 Tim. 2:11–13; Titus 3:1–8.

go wrong in church leadership, we'll eventually go wrong in salvation and sanctification.

Should we want to be leaders, considering that the work is so serious and consequential? "Yes," says Paul. "If anyone aspires to the office of overseer, he desires a noble task" (3:1). The leadership role of overseer in this context means shepherding souls, which is why Paul calls it "a noble task," meaning high and lofty work. Instead of shrinking back from such roles, Paul wants to see aspiration, a holy ambition for the task.

Christlike leaders know the enormity of the task,
and have the energy for the task.

"So, if I want to be a church leader, I should be a church leader?"
Not so fast.

Leadership Has High Qualifications 3:2–5

"Therefore an overseer must be above reproach" (3:2), which means he must have a good reputation. Criticism has nothing to stick to. This Teflon character results from two moral characteristics: self-control and family-control.

Self-control is demonstrated in being "the husband of one wife, sober-minded, self-controlled, respectable, hospitable, able to teach, not a drunkard, not violent but gentle, not quarrelsome, not a lover of money" (3:2–3). The leader is to be self-controlled in sexual matters, behavior, thinking, studying, addictive substances, conflict, speech, finances, and so on.

But self-management is not enough; the leader must also evidence family management. "He must manage his own household well, with all dignity keeping his children submissive, for if someone does not know how to manage his own household, how will he care for God's church?" (3:4–5). Leading well in the home indicates that someone will lead well in the church.

Self-control and family-control are evidence of Holy Spirit–control.

"This doesn't sound too hard."
You won't say that for long.

Leadership Starts Devilish Opposition 3:6–7

The devil wants to puncture leaders, which is why Paul says, "He must not be a recent convert, or he may become puffed up with conceit and fall into the condemnation of the devil" (3:6). A balloon is filled with hot air, rises high in the sky, and then bursts, resulting in a catastrophic fall. That's what the devil wants to do to us, and the way he does it is by giving us way too high thoughts about ourselves.

If he doesn't puncture leaders, he traps them. "Moreover, he must be well thought of by outsiders, so that he may not fall into disgrace, into a snare of the devil" (3:7). The devil wants to trap leaders because he knows that if he can bring down the leaders, then he can bring down the church and hinder the spread of the gospel.

The devil targets leaders because he knows leaders are targeting him.

Changing Our Story with God's Story

We worship Jesus as the perfect leader. He aspired to leadership and was up to the task. He was perfectly qualified by his perfect self-control and family-control. He defeated the most devilish opposition, puncturing and trapping the devil in the process.

Summary: What is Christlike leadership? *Desire to be a Christlike leader and develop Christlike character so that you can defend against devilish opposition.*

Question: How can you be (or support) a Christlike leader?

Prayer: Christ, my leader, make me like you so that I can lead your people like you.

God's servants don't get many tips, but they do get more trust.

Hear God's Story | Change Your Story | Tell the Story | Change Others' Stories

13

Table-Waiters Required

1 TIMOTHY 3:8-13

Given a choice, would you rather be a boss or a worker? A master or a servant? Most of us would choose to be in charge, wouldn't we? We view serving as a menial and even demeaning position with poor rewards.

So, if we were looking to employ people, the last word we'd use is *servant*, right? We know that would put people off from applying. But when God advertises for workers in the church, not only does he use the word *servant*; he uses the lowest servant word in the Bible: *deacon*.

So *why would anyone want to be a deacon or a servant*? First Timothy 3:8–13 explains that this kind of serving requires high qualifications and is highly rewarded. Although these verses are addressed to deacons specifically, everyone is called to be a servant in some way.

God Is Looking for Qualified Servants 3:8–12

Deacon means "servant" or "table-waiter." A deacon is to serve people's material needs so that pastors and elders are free to minister to spiritual needs (Acts 6:1–6). This, though, is not a menial job, as the following qualifications make clear.

When Paul says, "Deacons likewise must be dignified, not double-tongued, not addicted to much wine, not greedy for dishonest gain" (3:8), he's calling for men of good character.

When he adds, "They must hold the mystery of the faith with a clear conscience" (3:9), he's calling for men with good theology.

When he insists, "And let them also be tested first; then let them serve as deacons if they prove themselves blameless" (3:10), he's calling for men with a good record.

And when he warns, "Their wives likewise must be dignified, not slanderers, but sober-minded, faithful in all things. Let deacons each be the husband of one wife, managing their children and their own households well" (3:11–12), he's calling for men with good relationships.

These are the highest qualifications for the lowest position: good character, good theology, a good record, and good relationships.

Employers want good degrees, schools, connections, and looks,
but God wants good character, theology, records, and relationships.

"This kind of serving sounds like a lot of hard work. Is it worth it?"
Yes, because God encourages us with two rewards.

God Will Reward Faithful Servants 3:13

"For those who serve well as deacons gain a good standing for themselves and also great confidence in the faith that is in Christ Jesus" (3:13). Faithful servants will be rewarded with respect from God's people for their humble service, and with assured faith in Christ. Other servants will have greater trust in us, and we will have greater trust in Christ. Yes, the service is low, but the rewards are rich.

God's servants don't get many tips,
but they do get more trust.

Changing Our Story with God's Story

Jesus said he "came not to be served [*literally*, "deaconed"] but to serve [*literally*, "to deacon"] and to give [my] life as a ransom for many" (Mark 10:45). He also said, "I am among you as the one who serves" (Luke 22:27). Jesus was perfectly qualified for the highest leadership, yet he took the position of lowest service. He knew he would get no payment, but rather would pay with his life. Afterward, his deacon/servant death was rewarded with greater trust. No one served better, no one deserves better trust.

Are we prepared to take the position of Christlike lowliness and persevere in Christlike service with the assurance of Christlike rewards?

Summary: Why would anyone want to be a deacon or a servant? *Pursue God's high qualifications for lowly service, and your lowly service will be rewarded with the highest returns.*

Question: Do you want to be served or to serve? Would someone know the answer if they simply looked at your life?

Prayer: Lord of All Who Became Servant of All, make it my highest ambition to be the lowest servant.

Confessing our faith is cementing our faith.

 Hear God's Story | Change Your Story | Tell the Story | Change Others' Stories

14

Creeds Need Churches and Churches Need Creeds

1 TIMOTHY 3:14-16

What's the point of creeds and confessions? Aren't they just statements of academic theology with no practical relevance or value?

I must confess that when I was a young Christian, I not only thought that; I said it. But over the past thirty-plus years of following Christ, I've come to see that creeds and confessions are supremely relevant and extremely valuable. *What is the point of creeds and confessions?* First Timothy 3:14–16 provides two answers.

Creeds Need Churches 3:14–15

Paul desired to see Timothy but, aware that he might be delayed, wrote this letter to ensure order in the Ephesian church: "I hope to come to you soon, but I am writing these things to you so that, if I delay, you may know how one ought to behave in the household of God, which is the church of the living God, a pillar and buttress of the truth" (3:14–15).

In chapters 2 and 3 Paul teaches "how one ought to behave in the household of God" (3:15). The first two names he gives to the church, "the household of God . . . the church of the living God," remind us that God owns the church, and therefore he has the right to order it as he decides. The third name, "pillar and buttress of the truth," pictures the reality that God founded the church to establish, support, and promote the truth. Without the church, the truth would disintegrate and disappear in the world.

The church doesn't make up the truth,
but it does keep up the truth.

"So, creeds need churches. I thought churches needed creeds?"
That's true, too, which is why Paul next gives the church a creed to keep.

Churches Need Creeds 3:16

"Great indeed, we confess, is the mystery of godliness" (3:16). As in other places, Paul uses "mystery" in the sense of previously hidden but now revealed truths, and with these words he introduces the first "Apostles' Creed." What we today call the "Apostles' Creed" is a good creed, but it was probably not written by the apostles, as it's not mentioned until AD 390. The 1 Timothy 3:16 creed was recorded by Paul the apostle. It contains three pairs of truths that reveal and explain how godliness is produced.

The first pair says Christ was "manifested in the flesh, vindicated by the Spirit" (3:16). We confess that Christ was revealed and made known by his incarnation and his resurrection.

The second pair says he was "seen by angels, proclaimed among the nations" (3:16). We confess that Christ was witnessed to and reported about both in heaven and on earth.

The third pair asserts he was "believed on in the world, taken up in glory" (3:16). We confess that Christ was received on earth by faith and into heaven by the ascension. Six solid truths to settle, strengthen, and solidify the church and the Christian.

Confessing our faith is cementing our faith.

Changing Our Story with God's Story

The church depends on the truth for its existence and life; the truth depends on the church for its defense and proclamation. The particular truth Paul affirms in this passage is not just the truth that Christ is our Savior, but that Christ is our sanctifier. What's been revealed is that godliness is not so much the result of trying harder to be like Christ; it's more about believing better in Christ.

Confessing such a Christ inevitably brings us to loving Christ. We hear these six great confessional statements and join Paul in worshipful adoration when he says, "Great . . . is the mystery of godliness" (3:16).

Summary: What's the point of creeds and confessions? *Hold fast and hold up your confession of Christ to strengthen your faith, your holiness, and your church.*

Question: How can you use confessions and creeds to strengthen your faith, your holiness, and your church?

Prayer: Great God, thank you for revealing truths about Christ that were previously shrouded in mystery. Help me to confess these truths so that I and others in the church will be strong and strengthen others.

Hold fast God's word and world, and he will hold you fast by the word in the world.

 Hear God's Story | Change Your Story | Tell the Story | Change Others' Stories

15

Will He Hold Me Fast?

1 TIMOTHY 4:1–5

High-profile "deconversions" sometimes make the headlines. The old word for this is *apostasy*, a giving up of Christian truth and ethics. Whatever we call it, a number of prominent Christian authors, singers, personalities, podcasters, and even preachers have given up the faith.

Sometimes such departures from the faith shake our own faith. They raise questions such as, "Is Christianity true and reliable? Am I true and reliable? If such prominent Christians can't hold on to the truth, how will I? How do I keep my story from repeating theirs? *Will Jesus hold me fast?*"[1]

Paul anticipates departures from the faith. In 1 Timothy 4:1–5, he prepares Christians for this happening in the church, and guides us in how to hold on to our faith.

Apostates Reject God's Word and World 4:1–3

First Timothy 3 concluded with an inspiring confession of faith, but chapter 4 brings us back down to earth: "Now the Spirit expressly says that in later times some will depart from the faith" (4:1). "Later times" frequently refers to the whole period between Christ's first and second comings, the new covenant age, the times we are living in.

---

1 I recommend the song, "He Will Hold Me Fast," Getty Music Publishing (BMI) / Matthew Merker Music (BMI), 2013.

How does apostasy happen? What does it look like?

- *It is deceitful.* They depart from the faith by "devoting themselves to deceitful spirits" (4:1). They are duped into following lies.
- *It is demonic.* All false teaching, no matter how attractive, is "the teachings of demons" (4:1). It comes from Hell University.
- *It follows dulling.* They follow teachers with "the insincerity of liars whose consciences are seared" (4:2). Their consciences are dulled by teaching with their lips what they rejected in their hearts.
- *It despises God's gifts.* Apostates treat God's word and world with contempt. They contradict God's word and reject God's good gifts in the world. In this case, they "forbid marriage and require abstinence from foods that God created to be received with thanksgiving" (4:3).

Apostasy always begins with a rejection of God's word and God's world.

Departing from God begins with despising God.

"How do we not get swept away into apostasy?"
We must do the opposite. We must embrace God's word and world.

Believers Embrace God's Word and World 4:3–5

Believers have a much more positive attitude toward God's word and world.

- *We embrace God's good word.* Unlike unbelievers, believers are "those who believe and know the truth" (4:3).
- *We embrace God's good world.* If we embrace God's word, we will embrace God's world. God's good gifts of food and marriage are "to be received with thanksgiving.... For everything

created by God is good, and nothing is to be rejected if it is received with thanksgiving" (4:3–4).
- *We embrace God's world and word together.* Each of God's good gifts is "made holy by the word of God and prayer" (4:5). We bring God's word and God's world together. We don't separate them but unite them by prayer for our spiritual benefit.

As God embraces us with his word and world, we embrace him through his word and world.

Hold fast God's word and world,
and he will hold you fast by the word in the world.

Changing Our Story with God's Story

See how incredibly generous God is! He holds out his whole word and his whole world and says, "Have at it! Enjoy!" The more we see of God's goodness in his word and world, the more secure we will be in our faith. Let's gratefully enjoy all of God's many, varied, and good gifts, thank him for them, and use them as sanctifying influences in our lives. The best way to embrace God's word and world is to embrace Christ who is the Word and created the world.

Summary: Will Jesus hold me fast? *Embrace God's good word and God's good world in all their fullness as the best protection from apostasy.*

Question: Are you refusing any of God's good gifts?

Prayer: Good God, thank you for your good word and world, which you use to keep me in the faith.

Developing graces and gifts will do us more good than developing abs and biceps.

 Hear God's Story | Change Your Story | Tell the Story | Change Others' Stories

16

God's Healthcare Plan

1 TIMOTHY 4:6-8

A few years ago, I left my doctor's office with a bad report and a personal resolution to start eating better and exercising more. But I soon realized that it's a bit late to start on a health and fitness program when one is already sick. It would have been far better to start such habits when I was well. I wished I'd been proactive rather than reactive.

The same goes for our spiritual life: it's better to be proactive than reactive. Having warned about the dangers of the last times in 1 Timothy 4:1-5, in verses 6-8 Paul outlines a spiritual healthcare plan that is more about prevention than cure. It's a health plan that prepares believers for the last times so that they hold the faith when others are letting it go. So, *what's the Bible's spiritual healthcare plan?*

Godliness Requires Healthy Food 4:6-7

"If you put these things before the brothers, you will be a good servant of Christ Jesus, being trained in the words of the faith and of the good doctrine that you have followed" (4:6). "These things" are the nourishing truths that Paul just set before Timothy and which Timothy is to set before the church. A key part of the church's spiritual training is a diet of healthy words.

In contrast, Paul warns Timothy away from certain junk foods. "Have nothing to do with irreverent, silly myths" (4:7). Put spiritual superstitions, supplements, and speculations in the trash. Put time wasters in the waste disposal.

Junk food, junk soul; healthy food, healthy soul.

"Is that all we have to do, just eat good food and avoid junk food?"
No, we must also exercise.

Godliness Requires Healthy Exercise 4:7–8

In addition to training in the words of faith and good doctrine, Timothy is to "train [himself] for godliness" (4:7). *Train* is the word used for gymnastics exercise. Gymnasts work constantly on building their strength and stamina, no matter how much they have to suffer in the process. They do this to win gold. But for spiritual athletes, the aim is even higher; not gold but godliness.

What motivation does Paul give us? "For while bodily training is of some value, godliness is of value in every way, as it holds promise for the present life and also for the life to come" (4:8). Physical training has value. But spiritual training has far higher value.

Why? It has value not only for the present life, but also for the life to come. It benefits the soul. If we want bodily and spiritual health for all eternity, then we'll do bodily *and* spiritual exercise. Getting rid of sin is more important than getting rid of cellulite.

Developing graces and gifts will do us more
good than developing abs and biceps.

Changing Our Story with God's Story

All the top athletes have personal coaches because they know they need personal encouragement and accountability. They need someone beside them every day to spur them on and pick them up when they fall. Thankfully, spiritual athletes have the best coach in Jesus Christ. He is right beside us as we make choices between junk food and health food, between spiritual laziness and spiritual exercise. He was the best spiritual athlete in his day and therefore he not only knows the challenges we face but he knows how to overcome them too. And even when we fail, we can trust his faultlessness to cover our faultiness.

Summary: What's the Bible's spiritual healthcare plan? *Train every part of your body and soul, and especially your heart and mind, so that you will hold the faith in a faithless day.*

Question: What junk food can you replace with healthy food for the soul? What spiritual exercise can you add to your daily routine?

Prayer: Heavenly Trainer, thank you for providing food and exercise that help me to be spiritually healthy even when the plague of apostasy rages. Help me to eat well and exercise well so that I can hold the faith well and train others to do the same.

God gives us the pierced hands of Christ and the believing hands of faith.

 Hear God's Story | Change Your Story | Tell the Story | Change Others' Stories

17

The Real Reason We Don't Evangelize

1 TIMOTHY 4:9-10

How can we motivate greater evangelism? At the root of a lot of our evangelistic apathy and inactivity is the false idea that everyone will be saved. We might not say it out loud, and at times we may not even be conscious of it. But deep down, under many layers, many of us hold the false belief that everyone is going to heaven anyway. If we really believed everyone is going to hell unless they know Jesus, wouldn't we forget the embarrassment, the fear of rejection, and any sense of our insufficiency? We would be prepared to suffer, and we'd pour ourselves out for the task.

That's what Paul teaches in 1 Timothy 4:9-10: "The saying is trustworthy and deserving of full acceptance. For to this end we toil and strive, because we have our hope set on the living God, who is the Savior of all people, especially of those who believe" (4:9-10). Wait, did Paul just say that God is the Savior of all? Does God save everyone after all? Let's dig a little deeper into the two truths taught in this text to find truth that will motivate greater evangelism.

God Does Not Save Everyone 4:9-10

"We have our hope set on the living God, who is the Savior of all people, especially of those who believe" (4:10). This cannot mean that everyone who has ever lived is going to heaven regardless of their response to the gospel. That's not consistent with the rest of Scripture (e.g., Matt. 7:14). It doesn't explain Paul's missionary labors. Why would he "toil and strive," labor and suffer, if everyone is going to be saved anyway? The rest of this letter rejects universalism (1 Tim. 1:19; 2:5; 4:1), as do Paul's other letters (Rom. 11:5; 1 Cor. 16:22). And remember, Paul cautioned about apostasy at the beginning of chapter 4.

If God is Savior of all, then he is not Savior at all.

"So whom does God save?"
He saves believers alone.

God Saves Believers Alone 4:10

". . . the living God, who is the Savior of all people, especially of those who believe" (4:10). "All people" can mean "all kinds of people." "Especially" can mean "to be precise" or "in other words." Therefore, this verse teaches that God is the Savior of all kinds of people, specifically, all kinds of people who believe. God saves believers.

Faith has two hands. With the first hand it reaches out because it needs outside help, outside knowledge, outside power. It grasps and grips God's word because it helps us to grip God's Son. The other hand of faith receives. It receives Christ and all his benefits: forgiveness of sin, everlasting righteousness, salvation, and so on. But because we are born without spiritual arms, God gives us not only the one we are to believe in but the arms with which to believe. Praise God for giving us not only a salvation to believe in but a belief in his salvation. Hallelujah, what a Savior!

God gives us the pierced hands of Christ
and the believing hands of faith.

Changing Our Story with God's Story

Unless we really believe that God only saves believers in Christ, we will not serve Christ and we will not suffer for Christ. If we really believe God saves only those who believe in Jesus, we will labor and suffer until more sinners become believers in Jesus.

Summary: How can we motivate greater evangelism? *Believe that God saves only believers and not unbelievers to motivate spreading the faith to others and calling others to faith.*

Question: What gospel labor can you do today to call unbelievers to faith in Christ?

Prayer: Great Savior, thank you for your great salvation for a great number of great sinners. Strengthen me for great labors with your great gospel so that there will be a great multitude saved from hell and for heaven.

The young can be spiritual adults, and the old can be spiritual babies.

 Hear God's Story | Change Your Story | Tell the Story | Change Others' Stories

18

An Inspiring Call to Young Christians

1 TIMOTHY 4:11–16

Young Christians can sometimes be too brash ("The church needs me so much.") or too bashful ("I'm too young to be useful."). Timothy may have been on the bashful side of the church. He was hesitant and reluctant to step up, to serve, or to shepherd. He was slow, shy, and scared about what people would think if he was too forward for a young man (1 Tim. 4:12; 2 Tim. 1:7).

If that sounds like you, the apostle Paul has some stirring, encouraging, challenging, and motivating words for you in 1 Timothy 4:11–16. You can be an inspiring example to others. "How?" you ask. *"How can young Christians inspire others?"*

Young Christians Can Be Exemplary Characters 4:11–12

Older people tend to look down on the young. They don't ask them for advice, they don't listen to their voices, and they reject their opinions. But that shouldn't happen in the church. "Command and teach these things. Let no one despise you for your youth," Paul says to Timothy, who was about twenty years old (4:11–12).

Now, of course, we can't stop people from doing this to us if we're young, but young people can avoid giving others a reason to despise them, and they can resist being swayed or intimidated by negative perceptions from older people. How? "Set the believers an example in speech, in conduct, in love, in faith, in purity"

(4:12). Be an exemplary and outstanding Christian. Work toward well-rounded spiritual maturity in every area of Christian character. Christian usefulness starts with Christian character, and Christian character starts with Christ. Both usefulness and character result from spending time with Jesus.

The young can be spiritual adults and the old can be spiritual babies.

"Character is about being. What about doing? What can I actually do?" You can be exemplary teachers too.

Young Christians Can Be Exemplary Teachers 4:13–14

Paul says, "Until I come, devote yourself to the public reading of Scripture, to exhortation, to teaching. Do not neglect the gift you have, which was given you by prophecy when the council of elders laid their hands on you" (4:13–14).

Paul sees God-given teaching gifts in Timothy which were confirmed when he was installed as the young pastor of the Ephesus church. But they are there in seed form, not fully grown. Therefore, he urges Timothy to "practice these things, immerse yourself in them, so that all may see your progress" (4:15). Practice, immerse, progress; practice, immerse, progress. Be an example in the cultivation of grace and gifts, whatever your gifts may be.

Paul closes with a challenge and an encouragement. "Keep a close watch on yourself and on the teaching. Persist in this, for by so doing you will save both yourself and your hearers" (4:16). While inspiring others, remember to take care of your own spirituality. Don't get so focused on being a good example that you become a bad example. Keep your heart close to God and your teaching close to God's word. "Persist in this," never stop doing this, because a bad example destroys souls, while a good example saves souls.

Watch your heart and your head if you want to give a hand to others.

Changing Our Story with God's Story

Don't you love the way God encourages young people? Old Christians sometimes tell young Christians to sit down, but God says, "Stand up and stand out!" God's love for young Christians shines through Paul's love for young Timothy.

If we're old, let's never be discouraging despisers of the young. Whatever our age, let's be an encouraging example in grace and gifts, energizing others to be the same. A good example can be far more infectious than any virus, and result in life not death.

Summary: How can young Christians inspire others? *Inspire others with exemplary character and exemplary teaching.*

Question: How will you inspire the old (or the young) today?

Prayer: Inspiring God, you have inspired me to inspire others. Give me the grace and gifts I need to be inspired and inspiring.

Good relationships with others flow from a good relationship with God.

 Hear God's Story | Change Your Story | Tell the Story | Change Others' Stories

19

Four Skills in Personal Relationships

1 TIMOTHY 5:1-2

Many pastoral resignations are not caused by theological error, preaching incompetence, administrative neglect, or falling into immorality. They are caused by a lack of social skill, a lack of relational maturity, or, to use a modern phrase, a lack of emotional intelligence.

Even if you're not a pastor, you are still involved in personal ministry, and so you therefore need social skills and relational wisdom. You may think you just need better theology, better communication skills, better techniques, better examples, and so on. You may need all these, but as Paul teaches Timothy in 5:1–2, above all we need better personal relationships. *What are the most important skills in personal relationships?*

Personal Ministry Depends on Personal Godliness 4:12, 16

In the previous chapter, Paul emphasized the importance of personal godliness for Timothy's ministry. He called Timothy to be "an example in speech, in conduct, in love, in faith, in purity" (4:12).

He starts with personal godliness and then concludes with, "Persist in this, for by so doing you will save both yourself and your hearers" (4:16). He moves from personal godliness to personal relationships—those he ministers to personally.

If you want fruitfulness, start with godliness.

"Building on personal godliness, what relational skills do I need?" Here are four relational skills to work on.

Personal Ministry Depends on Relational Skill 5:1–2

"Do not rebuke an older man but encourage him as you would a father, younger men as brothers, older women as mothers, younger women as sisters, in all purity" (5:1–2). Here, Paul summarizes four simple relational skills for effective personal ministry.

Be adaptable. Paul's four categories of older men, younger men, older women, and younger women call us to adapt to whomever we are addressing. We do so by asking two basic questions: "Is this person older or younger than me?" and "Is this person male or female?" We're to relate to people differently depending on their age and sex.

Be familial. Treat older men as fathers, younger men as bothers, older women as mothers, and younger women as sisters. Don't treat the church as a company or as a kingdom, but as a family. And use healthy family relationships as a model for church family relationships.

Be an encourager. "Do not rebuke an older man but encourage him as you would a father" (5:1). This carries over to the other relationships too. Whatever else Paul is doing here, he's putting encouragement at the top of our list and rebuke way down the list. Encouragement is Plan A. Rebuke is Plan Z.

Be holy. When Paul instructs Timothy how to encourage younger women in personal ministry, he adds "in all purity" (5:2). He's aware that temptation is a reality even in ministry, and therefore adds this additional requirement that protects both men and women and causes them to flourish.

Good relationships with others flow from a good relationship with God.

Changing Our Story with God's Story

We see the love of God in these instructions as he organizes his church through Paul to be a holy, loving, encouraging family. He wants his people to be in loving personal relationships with each other. He wants these relationships to reflect his own relationship with his children: adaptable, familial, encouraging, and holy.

In the Gospels we see Christ's personal relationships flowing out of his personal godliness. He modeled these verses in his relationships with the old and the young, with men and women. He was so adaptable, familial, encouraging, and holy. We love him for his relational skills then with them and now with us.

Summary: What are the most important skills in personal relationships? *To be effective in Christlike personal ministry, be adaptable, familial, holy encouragers in personal relationships.*

Question: In which of these four relational skills can you grow in Christlikeness?

Prayer: Relational God, you are supremely skillful in personal relationships. Give me your relational skills so that I can be more like Christ in all my relationships.

The godly poor
take priority over
the poor in godliness.

 Hear God's Story | Change Your Story | Tell the Story | Change Others' Stories

20

God's Heart for the Poor

1 TIMOTHY 5:3–16

Should churches and Christians care for the material needs of the poor? If you're like me, at times you've grown frustrated when you've seen people waste money or become dependent on charity without taking personal responsibility.

At times, I've even thought about giving up on caring and helping altogether, but then I feel really guilty because I know there are poor people who desperately need help. How do we navigate this? Should we give to the poor? Which poor do we give to? *How do we help the poor without hurting them?* In 1 Timothy 5:3–16, the apostle Paul gives us three guidelines for Christian charity.

The Church Provides for the Poor 5:3, 16

Paul encouraged Timothy to provide for the needs of widows. "Honor widows who are truly widows. . . . Care for those who are truly widows" (5:3, 16). Although this is speaking specifically about widows, the Christian principle behind this teaching can be applied to all situations of poverty: single mothers, the terminally ill, the unemployed, those with disabilities, and so on.

The poor in spirit have a heart for the poor in pocket.

"Do we just give out money to every poor person?"
No, Paul sets up a screening process.

The Church Distinguishes between the Poor 5:3–13

Verses 3, 5, and 16 speak of providing for those who are "truly widows." The church clearly had too many widows receiving charity and not enough funds to provide for them all. Paul therefore urged Timothy to sift the applications and exercise discretion so that the truly poor got truly helped.

The first screening question is, *How old is the widow?* Verse 9 prioritizes those over the age of sixty, partly because they had less of a possibility of working or remarrying. Paul does not rule out younger widows getting some help and support, but it's not automatic.

The second screening question is, *How godly is the widow?* Aware of the church's limited resources, Paul calls the church to prioritize widows with a godly character and record (5:5–7, 9–13). Such a woman's godliness is evidenced in her God-centered hope and prayers: "She who is truly a widow, left all alone, has set her hope on God and continues in supplications and prayers night and day" (5:5) and in her good works: "Having a reputation for good works: if she has brought up children, has shown hospitality, has washed the feet of the saints, has cared for the afflicted, and has devoted herself to every good work" (5:10).

The godly poor take priority over the poor in godliness.

"Is the church fully responsible for poor Christians?"
No, it shares responsibility with others.

The Church Shares Responsibility for the Poor 5:14–15

Paul calls widows to take some responsibility for themselves. Paul critiques irresponsible widows who become idle gossips and pleasure-seekers, and in verses 14–15 directs them how to take some responsibility. The church is not responsible to provide for those acting irresponsibly. Paul also urges the family of widows to help (5:8, 16). The family is to step up and not leave it all to the church.

We take responsibility partly by calling to responsibility.

Changing Our Story with God's Story

Let's use this passage to fire up our love for the God of the widows, the God of the poor. We see this love throughout the Old Testament, with one whole book, Ruth, devoted to God's care for three widows.

We see God's heart in Jesus who resurrected a widow's son (Luke 7:11–17), commended a praying widow (Luke 18:1–18), and praised a giving widow (Luke 21:1–4). He rebuked devourers of widows' houses (Luke 20:47), and even made arrangements for his mother, probably a widow at this point, in his dying hour (John 19:25–27).

Summary: How do we help the poor without hurting them? *Reflect God's heart for the poor by providing for them in God's way.*

Question: What poor person will you help in this way, and how will you do it?

Prayer: Rich God, give me your beautiful heart for the poor and help me to follow your direction so that I help them rather than hurt them.

Leaders get greater provision and protection.

Hear God's Story | Change Your Story | Tell the Story | Change Others' Stories

21

The Pros and Cons of Leadership

1 TIMOTHY 5:17–25

Godly leaders can do tremendous good; ungodly leaders can do terrible harm. *How do we encourage godly leadership and discourage ungodly leadership in the church?*

Some men run to leadership for the privileges. Others run from leadership because of the responsibilities. Therefore, in 1 Timothy 5:17–25, Paul encourages the fearful with the privileges and deters the egomaniacs with the responsibilities.

Leaders Have Great Privileges 5:17–19

"Let the elders who rule well be considered worthy of double honor, especially those who labor in preaching and teaching. For the Scripture says, 'You shall not muzzle an ox when it treads out the grain,' and, 'The laborer deserves his wages'" (5:17–18). Those who *rule* well are to be honored by word and actions. Those who also *teach* well are to be doubly honored not only with words and actions, but also with material provision for their needs.

We not only provide for our spiritual leaders; we also protect them. "Do not admit a charge against an elder except on the evidence of two or three witnesses" (5:19). Leaders are more susceptible to false accusations, which can undermine their usefulness. Therefore, for their protection, a high standard of evidence is required before any charges are even considered.

*Leaders deserve provision and protection,
not poverty and penalty.*

"Provision and protection sound great! How can I be a leader?"
You probably need to hear the responsibilities first.

Leaders Have Great Responsibilities 5:20–25

With greater privileges come greater responsibilities. "As for those who persist in sin, rebuke them in the presence of all, so that the rest may stand in fear" (5:20). When sin is proven, leaders are to be more publicly and severely rebuked.

They are subject to higher standards here on earth because they will be subject to higher standards later at the judgment. "In the presence of God and of Christ Jesus and of the elect angels I charge you to keep these rules without prejudging, doing nothing from partiality" (5:21). Because they will one day be judged by God, they are to judge and administer justice without any prejudice or favoritism.

Leaders are to take their time in appointing others to leadership because if they appoint the wrong people, they'll share in the shame. "Do not be hasty in the laying on of hands, nor take part in the sins of others; keep yourself pure" (5:22).

Because Timothy suffered from stress-induced stomach problems, Paul prescribed a little medicinal wine: "No longer drink only water, but use a little wine for the sake of your stomach and your frequent ailments" (5:23).

Paul then gives Timothy some simple advice in leadership selection: "The sins of some people are conspicuous, going before them to judgment, but the sins of others appear later. So also good works are conspicuous, and even those that are not cannot remain hidden" (5:24–25). When it comes to the church judging men's fitness for leadership, some are ruled out immediately because of their obvious sins. The sins of others are hidden but will eventually become obvious. The good works of good candidates are always obvious.

*Leaders get greater provision and protection
but with greater rebuke, judgment, and stress.*

Changing Our Story with God's Story

Let's love godly leaders by seeing them as an expression of God's love for us. Let's thank God for giving us godly leaders who not only take the privileges but also accept the responsibilities. And worship God for providing Jesus Christ who set aside so many privileges in order to take the greatest responsibility. If anyone has earned the right to lead us, it's Jesus.

Summary: How do we encourage godly leadership and discourage ungodly leadership in the church? *Don't run to the privileges and away from the responsibilities but embrace both to model Jesus Christ in the shepherding of God's flock.*

Question: How can you lead better or support your church's leaders better?

Prayer: Best Leader, lead me into becoming a better leader by making me a better follower of Jesus.

Our daily work has eternal consequences.

 Hear God's Story | Change Your Story | Tell the Story | Change Others' Stories

22

Witnessing at Work

1 TIMOTHY 6:1–2

How can I be a witness? I don't do open-air preaching; I don't hand out tracts; I don't go door to door; I don't talk to strangers about the gospel; and I'm not a missionary. How can I witness? The good news is that we have a ready-made, natural mission field much closer to home: our workplace.

The workplace? *How can I be a witness in the workplace?* I get how to be a witness at home and in my neighborhood, but how do I witness at work? Am I to go around the office or factory preaching to everyone, giving them texts and Christian books? Paul trains us for workplace evangelism in 1 Timothy 6:1–2.

Hard Work Helps the Gospel in the World 6:1

"Let all who are under a yoke as bondservants regard their own masters as worthy of all honor" (6:1). In the previous chapter, Paul discussed honoring women, honoring widows, and honoring elders. Now he comes to honoring employers. And he takes the hardest employment situation possible, that of slavery, being a slave to a master. Paul is not accepting slavery as right, but rather is working within the social system of the day.

Whether the masters were bad or good, they were to be respected. While Paul urged slaves to make use of an opportunity for freedom, in the meantime they were not to rebel but to work hard and speak well of their masters. Why? "So that the name of

God and the teaching may not be reviled" (6:1). Like them, we are to live and work so that God is glorified not tarnished and the gospel is helped not hindered. Our work can be an important part of our witness.

Our daily work has eternal consequences.

"I wish I could work for a Christian; then I wouldn't need to work so hard." That's not Paul's logic. He actually demands more of us if we have Christian employers.

Hard Work Helps the Gospel in the Church 6:2

How do we witness in a Christian workplace? "Those who have believing masters must not be disrespectful on the ground that they are brothers" (6:2). Spiritual equality in the church does not mean vocational equality in the workplace. Just because someone's our brother in the Christian community, doesn't mean we treat him like a buddy in the workplace.

Indeed, having a Christian boss means harder work not slacker work. "Rather they must serve all the better" (6:2). Although Christian masters will treat you better than non-Christian masters, you are not to take advantage of that for your benefit but rather take advantage of it for their benefit.

"Since those who benefit by their good service are believers and beloved" (6:2). Having Christian employers is a greater incentive to work harder. They are fellow believers and also beloved by God. The more profit they make in their business, the more money there is for gospel work.

We are busier because they are believers.
They are benefitted because they are beloved.

Changing Our Story with God's Story

We can express our love for God and for the lost by the way we work, by our work ethic. When we've done a hard day's work and earned our employer profit or benefitted others by our work, we've just been a powerful gospel witness. If we witness at work through our work, we'll often find that our work will open people's eyes and ears to the gospel.

Let's love our Lord Jesus who worked so hard and served so well to benefit the world and especially his beloved people. No one worked harder, no one witnessed better.

Summary: How can I be a witness in the workplace? *Witness well by working well, and you'll do good in both the world and the church.*

Question: How can you glorify God better at work?

Prayer: My Heavenly Boss, give me strength to work hard so I can witness hard in my workplace.

A lover of controversy is a hater of souls.

 Hear God's Story | Change Your Story | Tell the Story | Change Others' Stories

23

Fake News That's Fatal News

1 TIMOTHY 6:3–5

We live in a dangerous world, don't we? I write this while we're still in the middle of a global pandemic and as global conflicts are worsening. Violent extremism on the right and the left threatens democracy. How do we protect ourselves and our loved ones in this dangerous world?

In truth, there's something far more dangerous than viruses, war, and extremism in the world. It's killed millions, even billions, and it's still doing so today. It's false teaching about religion. It has destroyed and damned more people than any other danger.

We must take defensive measures to protect ourselves and our loved ones, and the first step is recognizing false teaching. If we don't know what we're dealing with and what to look out for, we're going to be extremely vulnerable. *How can we identify false teachers?* In 1 Timothy 6:3–5 Paul highlights four marks of false teachers.

False Teachers Contradict the Scriptures

"If anyone teaches a different doctrine and does not agree with the sound words of our Lord Jesus Christ and the teaching that accords with godliness . . ." (6:3). Anything that differs from the words of Scripture or our Savior is false, fraudulent, and fake, because it doesn't produce godliness but devilishness.

Fake news is fatal news.

"Why do false teachers do what they do?"
Personal vanity.

False Teachers Are Proud

"He is puffed up with conceit and understands nothing" (6:4). False teachers are vain and self-centered. They are proud of their knowledge, yet know nothing worth knowing. Paul punctures their boastful bubble by telling them, "You know a lot but understand nothing."

False teachers are self-inflated but are easily deflated.

"What do they teach?"
Divisive lies.

False Teachers Major on Minors

False teachers know a lot about little and little about a lot. They have "an unhealthy craving for controversy and for quarrels about words" (6:4). And what's the result of that? It produces "envy, dissension, slander, evil suspicions, and constant friction among people who are depraved in mind and deprived of the truth" (6:4–5). They specialize in limited areas and weaponize that to portray themselves as knowledgeable and right and everyone else as ignorant and wrong.

A lover of controversy is a hater of souls.

"What's their aim?"
Money.

False Teachers Are Greedy

"Imagining that godliness is a means of gain" (6:5). Whatever differs among false teachers, this unites them all: they are greedy and use religion primarily to make money and view money as a proof of godliness.

We make disciples not dollars.

Changing Our Story with God's Story

Doesn't this make us love Jesus more? He was truth enfleshed. Not only did he teach the word perfectly, but he is the perfect word. His teaching is the only hope of godliness. "You will know the truth, and the truth will set you free" (John 8:32). He said, "Learn from me, for I am gentle and lowly in heart, and you will find rest for your souls" (Matt. 11:29). He knew more truth than anyone else and yet was humble about it. He focused on majors and used the truth to unite people. He had no desire to gain wealth; he cared only for the gain of his hearers.

Later in this chapter, Paul reflects on this section and warns, "Flee these things" (6:11). Run away from them as fast as you possibly can. Run from falsehood, and run to the truth of Jesus, because your life—your spiritual life, and your eternal life—depends upon it.

Summary: How can we identify false teachers? *Know the truth to identify the actions and characteristics that don't match the truth and run from them.*

Question: Whom can you rescue from deadly error with this passage?

Prayer: God of Truth, thank you for preserving me in the midst of so much deadly false teaching. You've given me the truth, you've given me true teachers of truth, and you've kept me in the truth.

Personal gain is not godliness, but true godliness is gain.

 Hear God's Story | Change Your Story | Tell the Story | Change Others' Stories

24

Get-Rich-Slowly Scheme

1 TIMOTHY 6:6–8

I worked in the financial services industry in my early twenties and met lots of people with lots of money. I often envied them. But even though I was not a Christian at the time, I discerned that even the richest people never had enough. They were rich by any objective standard, but they didn't *feel* rich. They felt that they needed more to not only be rich but to *feel* rich.

Even if we're not rich, most of us want to be just a bit richer. Yet no matter how much more we get, it's never enough. We never *feel* rich. *How can we feel rich?* In 1 Timothy 6:6–8, Paul explains not only how to *be* rich but also how to *feel* rich.

We Get Rich through Godliness 6:6

Paul condemned the false teachers for using godliness for personal gain (6:5). Now Paul commends godliness as gain. "But godliness with contentment is great gain" (6:6). We'll look at contentment below, but notice for now how Paul redefines the whole concept of wealth. Godliness is not a way *to* riches but *is* riches. If we are godly, we are rich. If we walk with God, we have a rich lifestyle, because if we have God, we have everything.

Personal gain is not godliness,
but true godliness is gain.

"OK, but how do I feel rich?"
Feel rich by feeling content.

We Feel Rich through Contentment 6:6–8

While godliness makes us rich, it's contentment that makes us *feel* rich. "Godliness with contentment is great gain" (6:6).

How do we get contentment? Paul's already taken us halfway there by his redefinition of riches as godliness, not gold. Contentment takes us the whole way there by giving us two labels.

The first label is for putting on what we don't have. The label is: "If we have food and clothing, with these we will be content" (6:8). We can shorten that to "I have enough." "I may not have this or that, but I have enough. I have all I need." Put this sticker "I have enough" on your house, your car, your wardrobe, and your bank account, and watch your contentment multiply.

The second label is: "For we brought nothing into the world, and we cannot take anything out of the world" (6:7). Let's shorten it to: "Nothing in. Nothing out." We come into this world empty, and we leave this world empty.

Put this label on all possessions. "Nothing in. Nothing out." Put this label on all commercials. "Nothing in. Nothing out." Put this label on all people. No matter how rich someone might be, "Nothing in. Nothing out." Put this label on all things at all times:

- When we get something we always wanted: "Nothing in. Nothing out."
- When we get too attached to something we have: "Nothing in. Nothing out."
- When we lose something we treasured: "Nothing in. Nothing out."

That way, we can use "nothing" to get everything we need.

Even if we get everything, we go out with nothing.

Changing Our Story with God's Story

Let's praise God for freeing us from the bondage of wanting more and more yet never feeling it's enough. Let's thank him for helping us redefine godliness as riches and for providing these two contentment labels: "I have enough" and "Nothing in. Nothing out."

And let's love Jesus more, who, though he had nothing, he had everything. He didn't even have a place to sleep (Matt. 8:20), yet he was always perfectly content. Indeed, he gave up immeasurable wealth and became poor so that we would not only be rich but feel rich (2 Cor. 8:9). What a Savior!

Summary: How do we feel rich? *Get rich and feel rich through godliness plus contentment because godliness + contentment = great wealth.*

Question: How will you invest in contentment?

Prayer: Rich God, thank you for supplying all my needs and making me feel rich even when I'm not materially rich.

The love of money gives us some things, but it takes away everything worth having.

 Hear God's Story | Change Your Story | Tell the Story | Change Others' Stories

25

A Good Friend Becomes Our Worst Enemy

1 TIMOTHY 6:8–10

Money can be a good friend. It gives comforts and opportunities to us and our families. It supports churches and charities as they minister to the spiritually and financially poor. Money can be such a good friend that it's no wonder we desire its company in our lives.

But the *love* of money is our worst enemy. As Paul says in 1 Timothy 6:10, "The love of money is a root of all kinds of evil." How do we make money our friend without letting it become our enemy? How do we desire money without being destroyed by it? *How do we prevent the love of money from taking root in our lives?* Paul gives us two weed-killing truths in this passage.

The Love of Money Is the Root of Moral Evil 6:8–9

"But those who desire to be rich fall into temptation" (6:9). The love of money makes us do wrong things in order to get more money. Once we've fallen into temptation like that, it's not so easy to get up again because we've not just fallen on the ground, we've fallen "into a snare" (6:9). The love of money traps us. It gets a grip and won't let go.

The love of money doesn't come alone. It brings lots of friends along with it. Their names are "many senseless and harmful desires" (6:9). The love of money stimulates multiple other irrational and damaging desires that "plunge people into ruin and destruction" (6:9).

If we sow money-love, we are sowing self-destruction.

"If this harvest of moral evil is not enough to deter us from the love of money, what else will work?" Paul adds one more evil.

The Love of Money Is the Root of Spiritual Evil 6:10

"It is through this craving that some have wandered away from the faith and pierced themselves with many pangs" (6:10). The yearning for more money is at the root of many giving up the faith. Paul uses an interesting word here: *wandered*. Paul doesn't say, "They decided to leave the faith." No, they "wandered." They began slowly moving away from the faith. It wasn't anything dramatic or obvious. It was slow, almost casual; but inch by inch, turn by turn, they left the faith. When the love of money takes over, it takes our faith away.

Some wanderings are not so dangerous, but this one is fatal. They "pierced themselves with many pangs" (6:10). The love of money results in self-harm. It's like cutting our souls. If you doubt that, check out the "Where are they now?" pictures of those who were rich and famous ten or twenty years ago. If that's what the love of money does to our bodies, what does it do to our souls? If we could see our hearts, we would see multiple spears, arrows, and knives sticking out of them.

The love of money gives us some things, it but takes away everything worth having.

Changing Our Story with God's Story

While these two truths can kill many of the weeds that spring from the love of money, only another love can get to the deepest roots, and that's love for God. Love for God is the root of all moral, spiritual, and eternal good. If we sow love for God, it will produce an abundant, beautiful, healthy harvest in our lives. That's why Jude tells believers living in the midst of apostasy, "Keep yourselves in the love of God" (Jude 21). Love God the Father, God the Son, and God the Spirit for a triple-power weed-killer of money-love.

Summary: How do we prevent the love of money from taking root in our lives? *Sow love for God to root out the worst weeds and to produce a harvest of holiness, safety, faithfulness, and eternal life.*

Question: How are you cultivating love for God in your life?

Prayer: Lovable God, help me to love you much more than money so that I can produce fruit not weeds.

If we've run
to Christ,
we'll run away
from sin.

 Hear God's Story | Change Your Story | Tell the Story | Change Others' Stories

26

The Four *F*'s of the Christian Life

1 TIMOTHY 6:11–12

According to Christian publishers, the most popular Christian books are those on the Christian life. Yet the number and variety of such books tell us there's a lot of confusion about what the Christian life really is. Otherwise, why would we need so many books? So, *what is it to live as a Christian?*

As Paul comes to the end of his first letter to Timothy, a letter that's been complicated and controversial, he refocuses Timothy on the basics of the Christian life. This is a great help to us, as well, in the midst of life's complications and church controversies. Paul sums up the Christian life with four *f*'s.

Flee the False 6:11

First, we need to learn to run away. "But as for you, O man of God, flee these things" (6:11). "These things" are the issues Paul raised in this letter: fear of man, the love of controversy, division, and money. Turn your back on these things and run as fast as you can in the opposite direction. Run as if you're being chased by the devil.

If we've run to Christ, we'll run away from sin.

"So, am I just running away all the time?"
No, we also have to run toward something.

Follow Faithfulness 6:11

We run away from the false and toward faithfulness: "Pursue righteousness, godliness, faith, love, steadfastness, gentleness" (6:11). Paul defines faithfulness in three pairs of balanced spirituality:

- "Righteousness" is faithfulness in our relationships with people, whereas "godliness" is faithfulness in our relationship with God.
- "Faith" and "love" are paired a few times in 1 Timothy as each feeds the other.
- "Steadfastness" is tough patience, whereas "gentleness" is tender patience.

Spirituality requires a constant balancing act if we are to avoid falling into dangerous extremes.

Follow faithfulness, and you'll be a faithful follower.

"What about the attacks on Christian ethics and doctrine?
Do I just watch those get attacked?"
No, we have to fight.

Fight for the Faith 6:12

"Fight the good fight" (6:12) is literally "agonize the good agony." What have we to agonize for? "The faith," which here means the doctrine that faith believes. Fighting for God's truth is a tough and traumatic fight, but it's always a "good fight." When you're fighting for God's truth in the area of doctrine or ethics, do it with all you have and do it to win. You'll be wounded, but you'll win.

Fighting for the faith is good for our faith and the faith.

"Is all this worth it?"
The fourth f makes it all worthwhile and
supplies the energy for the other three f's.

Fasten on to Heaven 6:12

"Take hold of the eternal life to which you were called" (6:12). Hold the hope of heaven more tightly, more confidently, more certainly, more hopefully, and more happily. Fasten yourself to this hope by daily exercising this hope.

Grab heaven with both hands,
or hell will grab you with both hands.

Changing Our Story with God's Story

I love the simplicity and clarity God provides here through Paul's four *f*'s. Flee, follow, fight, fasten. That's it. Whatever else you do, do this. Don't you love the God who simplifies and clarifies things for us in such a complex and confusing world? Let's praise him for giving us not just a teacher of these truths in Paul, but a model of them in Christ. He lived the four *f*'s flawlessly and, in doing so, covers all our flaws and fails.

Summary: What is it to live as a Christian? *Keep the Christian life simple by fleeing faster, following closer, fighting harder, and fastening tighter.*

Question: Which of the four *f*'s do you have to work on?

Prayer: Faithful God, help me to be faithful to you by fleeing faster, following fully, fighting fiercer, and fastening firmly.

Christ's witness motivates Christian witness.

Hear God's Story | Change Your Story | Tell the Story | Change Others' Stories

27

God the Master Motivator

1 TIMOTHY 6:12-14

Motivational speakers motivate people by their speeches. They inspire people to dream big dreams and do great deeds. We sometimes need someone like that in our lives. When we get discouraged in the face of huge challenges, we need someone to come alongside us and encourage us.

Paul played that motivational role in Timothy's life by encouraging him in the face of hostile opposition (6:1-10) and by inspiring him to take on the immense challenge he'd just read in the four imperatives of verses 11-12: flee falsehood, follow faithfulness, fight for the faith, and fasten on to eternal life.

Paul summed it up with "I charge you . . . to keep the commandment unstained and free from reproach" (6:13-14). Great opposition, a great challenge, and a great charge. Paul, therefore, gave Timothy four motivations based upon four sets of eyes. *What can motivate gospel obedience in the face of great opposition?* Let's learn from God the master motivator.

Many Saw Your Confession 6:12

The first motivation is, "You made the good confession in the presence of many witnesses" (6:12). Paul reminds Timothy of his public testimony when he was converted to Christ and then ordained to the ministry. "Many eyes saw your confession, Timothy, and these eyes are upon you. Gospel friends are watching you and desperately need you to succeed."

Public confession motivates public confidence.

"But I'm being threatened on all sides."
Paul points us to God's eyes.

God Sees the Threats 6:13

The second motivation is that God is present and ruling over all life: "I charge you in the presence of God, who gives life to all things" (6:13). "Timothy, you are not alone; you are in God's presence. And God not only protects and sustains your life, but also can take away the life of your enemies." Timothy could go into the middle of threatening situations with the gospel because God was present with him.

God's presence motivates gospel presence.

"I wish I had an example to inspire me to this courage."
That's why Paul points Timothy to Jesus.

Christ Sees Your Witness 6:13

This charge is also given "in the presence of . . . Christ Jesus, who in his testimony before Pontius Pilate made the good confession" (6:13). Timothy was not only in God's presence in general but Christ's presence in particular. Paul was saying, "Timothy, the Christ who gave such a good example of standing for the faith in the face of the worst opposition is seeing you and urging you to follow his example."

Christ's witness motivates Christian witness.

"When will all the opposition come to an end?"
When all will see Christ.

All Will See Christ 6:14

Timothy was to "keep the commandment unstained and free from reproach until the appearing of our Lord Jesus Christ" (6:14). We see Jesus by faith just now, but soon all will see Jesus with their own eyes. He will appear when he comes to judge the world. Anticipate his visibility on that great day of triumph to encourage you to make Christ visible today by your witness.

Christ's future coming motivates our present courage.

Changing Our Story with God's Story

God is the master motivator. He doesn't just give us commands; he gives us courage. He doesn't just instruct us; he inspires us. Don't you love that? Christianity is such a reasonable faith. It's full of reasons for faith and obedience. God could simply command obedience, but he does much more than that. He explains it and encourages us in it. He treats us as rational creatures, not robotic clones. We worship the master-motivator.

Summary: What can motivate gospel obedience in the face of great opposition? *Motivate your Christian life with the master motivator's use of the church's eyes, God's eyes, Christ's eyes, and the whole world's eyes.*

Question: Which of these motivations will you use to motivate gospel witness today?

Prayer: Master Motivator, move me to obedience with all the eyes I need.

Worship doesn't just help us feel good; it helps us fight for good.

 Hear God's Story | Change Your Story | Tell the Story | Change Others' Stories

28

Winning by Worshiping

1 TIMOTHY 6:15–16

As we come to the end of 1 Timothy, we can identify more with timid Timothy. We feel his fear as we face our own high callings and scary challenges.

However, we're also encouraged by the number of tools, weapons, strategies, and tactics we've acquired to help us answer our callings and overcome our challenges. Our confidence is strengthening and our cowardice is weakening.

We want to be gallant, gutsy, and gritty in the Lord's service. But we need one last boost. *How can we get a super-shot of tough tenacity?* Paul takes out two vials in 1 Timothy 6:15–16, one labeled *the character of God* and the other *the worship of God*.

The Character of God Encourages Us 6:15–16

Fight hard because God is "the blessed and only Sovereign, the King of kings and Lord of lords" (6:15), and therefore the outcome is certain. God is invincible, meaning this is not a kamikaze mission.

That's because God "alone has immortality" (6:16). Because death cannot touch him, he will outlast and outlive all opposition. God is immortal, and therefore he can give immortality to those who sacrifice their mortality in his service.

Moreover, God "dwells in unapproachable light, whom no one has ever seen or can see" (6:16). "Timothy, the world is a dark and scary place, but look up by faith and see the beautiful holiness and the holy beauty of God. In a yukky mucky world, keep your eyes on the immaculate God."

Yes, we have a great calling and face great challenges, but the invincible, immortal, immaculate God is greater than them all.

Dwell in God's light by faith, and you can dwell in the dark world with courage.

"So, all I need is better theology?"
No, you also need better worship.

The Worship of God Encourages Us 6:16

Paul's theology always leads him to worship. He can't help himself. As he meditates on God's character and describes God to Timothy, his heart is warmed, his spirit is stirred, his emotions are raised, and he eventually bursts forth with: "To him be honor and eternal dominion. Amen" (6:16).

Everything Paul has written in the past six chapters has been about getting Timothy "to him," to the encouraging experience of worshiping in the presence of God. Theology and practice are the fuel for worship, but worship is the fire. It burns up fear, cowardice, and timidity. It ignites spiritual graces, gifts, and godliness. It energizes the soul and shines through the life of the worshiper. It brings God to the soul and the soul to God. "To him be honor and eternal dominion. Amen" (6:16). We worship our way to war.

Worship doesn't just help us feel good; it helps us fight for good.

Changing Our Story with God's Story

We must always move from learning the Bible to loving the Bible and the God of the Bible. Learning is great, but loving is greater. We must get from head to heart. Learning is the way to loving, but loving is a far greater power than learning. We can't bypass learning and go straight to loving, but neither can we stop at learning. Indeed, the more we love, the more we will want to learn. It's a virtuous circle. Learning gives us the weapons of spiritual warfare, but loving gives us the courage to actually fight with them.

Summary: How can we get a super-shot of tough tenacity? *Encourage yourself in the Lord with the character of God and the worship of God, and then you'll have not only the weapons but the courage to use them.*

Question: What challenge are you facing, and what aspect of God's character can inject courage into your trembling heart?

Prayer: Blessed and Only Sovereign, the King of kings and Lord of lords, use your character and worship to equip me for victory over my challenges.

If we're tempted to want more money, we're asking for more temptation.

Hear God's Story | Change Your Story | Tell the Story | Change Others' Stories

29

The Pros and Cons of Being Rich

1 TIMOTHY 6:17–21

"Wealth is wonderful and makes us wonderful." That's the message the media bombards us with every day. No wonder so many of us want to be rich. But is wealth all it's made out to be? Sure, there are advantages to being wealthy, but are there any disadvantages? *What are the pros and cons of being rich?*

Having reframed and redefined riches (6:1–10), Paul then reframes and redefines the rich (6:17–21). He highlights both the advantages and disadvantages of being rich, then surprises us with a closing definition of who is truly rich. By adding these verses as a postscript to his letter, just after his fitting climax of praise (6:15–16), Paul underlines how a wrong view of riches cannot coexist with a right view of worship or a right approach to ministry.

The Rich Have Extra Temptations 6:17

The rich face three unique temptations. First, they are tempted with pride. "As for the rich in this present age, charge them not to be haughty" (16:17). The wealthy often look down on the poor as inferior people.

Second, they are tempted to trust in their riches. That's why Timothy is to charge them "not to set their hopes on the uncertainty of riches, but on God" (6:17). Money can become our comfort and security. We end up trusting our accountant rather than our Creator.

Third, they are tempted to self-sufficiency. Because the rich tend to think that they are entirely self-made, they are to remember that it is "God, who richly provides us with everything to enjoy" (6:17). They are God-made not self-made.

If we're tempted to want more money,
we're asking for more temptation.

"Are there no positives in having wealth?"
Yes, there are some huge positives.

The Rich Have Extra Opportunities 6:18–19

The rich "are to do good, to be rich in good works" (6:18). Wealth gives the wealthy a great opportunity to invest in others and frees them from paid work to engage in voluntary works for the good of others. The rich are "to be generous and ready to share" (6:18), because they have money surplus to their needs and therefore have extra opportunities to give to others.

In doing this they are "storing up treasure for themselves as a good foundation for the future, so that they may take hold of that which is truly life" (6:19). This does not mean that charitable works earn us eternal life. It means that we are to keep our minds on the world to come and use our resources with a view to doing eternal good.

The rich have more resources and therefore more responsibilities.

"If I'm not rich, then there's nothing for me here."
Look at who is truly wealthy.

The Rich Are Redefined 6:20–21

Paul closes his letter by reminding us of who is truly wealthy. Timothy is to "guard the deposit entrusted to [him]" (6:20). Because the gospel is so valuable, those who have it are truly rich, and they protect it as they would a bar of gold. If we do so, we will "avoid the irreverent babble and contradictions of what is falsely called 'knowledge,' for by professing it some have swerved from the faith" (6:20–21).

Timothy is to guard God's gold of truth and avoid the fool's gold of error—even if it comes from the wealthy—because it leads people astray.

The poor in spirit have the kingdom of heaven.

Changing Our Story with God's Story

Unlike people, God does not relate to us depending on how much money we have. Jesus warned the rich and lifted up the poor. He valued faith more than finance, dependence more than dollars.

Summary: What are the pros and cons of being rich? *Reframe wealth to protect from its dangers, develop its opportunities, and value those who are spiritually rich.*

Question: How can you use any excess wealth to bless others?

Prayer: Rich God, thank you for sharing your riches with me, both material and spiritual. Guide me so that I use your gifts for the benefit and blessing of others here and hereafter.

2 TIMOTHY

Remember to pray, pray to remember, and remember in prayer.

 Hear God's Story | Change Your Story | Tell the Story | Change Others' Stories

30

Look Back to Look Forward

2 TIMOTHY 1:1-7

Fear is facing the future without faith. When we look ahead without looking up, it's no wonder that we look within and experience dread. *How do we face the future with faith instead of fear?* That's the question timid Timothy was asking, and Paul answered it in this second letter to him.

Paul hints at the answer in his initial greeting by pointing Timothy backward to God's promises so he can find God's grace, mercy, and peace for the future. "Paul, an apostle of Christ Jesus by the will of God according to the promise of the life that is in Christ Jesus, to Timothy, my beloved child: Grace, mercy, and peace from God the Father and Christ Jesus our Lord" (1:1–2). Paul then fleshes out this spiritual strategy of looking back in faith to look forward in faith.

We Remember One Another 1:3–5

We can remember in a way that fills us with regret and bitterness. But when Paul remembers Timothy, it fills him with gratitude: "I thank God whom I serve, as did my ancestors, with a clear conscience, as I remember you" (1:3). How does Paul remember Timothy?

Paul remembers Timothy in prayer: "As I remember you constantly in my prayers night and day" (1:3). Prayer is the best way to remember people. It's not just bringing someone to mind but bringing someone to God. When Timothy comes to Paul's mind, his immediate thought is to come to God with Timothy. Paul remembers Timothy in prayer, and prayer reminds Paul of Timothy. So much so, that he can't remember Timothy without praying and he can't pray without remembering Timothy.

Paul remembers Timothy's tears: "As I remember your tears, I long to see you, that I may be filled with joy" (1:4). When Paul remembers his tear-filled departure from Timothy, he longs for a joy-filled reunion with him.

Paul remembers Timothy's genuine faith: "I am reminded of your sincere faith" (1:5). When he reflects on it, Paul enjoys thinking about how Timothy's beautiful faith was faithfully passed down in his family. It "dwelt first in your grandmother Lois and your mother Eunice and now, I am sure, dwells in you as well" (1:5).

Remember to pray, pray to remember, and remember in prayer.

"Why did Paul let us look into his memory?"
To prompt Timothy and us to look into our own memory.

We Remind One Another 1:6–7

Paul remembers Timothy because he wants Timothy to remember. Paul's remembering should remind Timothy of the spiritual gifts God had given to him: "For this reason I remind you to fan into flame the gift of God, which is in you through the laying on of my hands" (1:6). Paul points Timothy back to his ordination as a pastor to jog his memory about how God had owned that moment and him by pouring out his Spirit upon him.

Why is it so important that Timothy bring this experience back to his memory? Because, in Paul's absence, he might have been feeling lonely and scared. Such feelings would be totally unnecessary and irrational, Paul says, "For God gave us a spirit not of fear but of power and love and self-control" (1:7).

Paul remembers Timothy and wants Timothy to remember the Holy Spirit. Paul is now absent from Timothy's life, so the apostle reminds him that the Holy Spirit is still present. Paul has not forgotten Timothy, and the Holy Spirit has not forgotten Timothy. By remembering the Spirit, Timothy can replace fear with courage, weakness with power, withdrawal with love, and panic with self-control.

Look back at past blessings to look forward to future blessings.

Changing Our Story with God's Story

This looking back to look forward was the constant posture of our Lord Jesus. How many times he looked backward at God's blessings to look forward with new courage in his mission.

Summary: How do we face the future with faith instead of fear? *Look back with gratitude to look forward with courage.*

Question: What memory of past blessings can help you face today with courage?

Prayer: Eternal God, remind me of your past blessings so that I can look forward with courage instead of fear.

Our doing is only done by God's doing.

 Hear God's Story | Change Your Story | Tell the Story | Change Others' Stories

31

Suffering without Shame

2 TIMOTHY 1:8–18

Suffering shames. That's why the devil loves persecution. He knows that making us suffer for Christ can make us ashamed of Christ. He turns up the heat on Christians to chill our boldness so that we lose our courage to speak and live the truth. *How can we stop being ashamed of the gospel?* In 1 Timothy 2:8–14, Paul helps Timothy shed shame.

Remember What Jesus Did 1:8–10

"Therefore do not be ashamed of the testimony about our Lord, nor of me his prisoner, but share in suffering for the gospel by the power of God" (1:8). How? Paul knew that the way to get Timothy back to gospel work was by focusing his attention on Christ's gospel work. "[He] saved us and called us to a holy calling, not because of our works but because of his own purpose and grace, which he gave us in Christ Jesus before the ages began" (1:9).

Paul doesn't berate Timothy into courage or shame him out of shame. Rather, he points to God's gospel initiative "which now has been manifested through the appearing of our Savior Christ Jesus, who abolished death and brought life and immortality to light through the gospel" (1:10). Timothy may have thought death was the worst-case scenario, but Paul insists that death is now the best-case scenario. Christ's death changed death so much that it's now the way to life and immortality.

Christ died the worst death, so we can die the best death.

"But God's purpose and Christ's fulfilment of it were in the past. What about the present?"
Jesus is still working today.

Remember What Jesus Is Doing 1:11–14

Although gospel workers will be gospel sufferers (1:11–12), gospel suffering does not have to produce gospel shame: "But I am not ashamed" (1:12).

How is this possible? How can Paul suffer without shame? "For I know whom I have believed, and I am convinced that he is able to guard until that day what has been entrusted to me" (1:12). Christ's gospel work is not just in the past but in the present. He is at work securing Paul's faith day by day and will do so until the very end. Again, Paul is pointing Timothy not to what he must do for Christ but to what Christ is doing for Paul.

Jesus isn't done; he's still doing.

"Jesus has done and is doing. What can I do?"
Follow and guard.

Remember What You Must Do 1:13–14

Having highlighted what Christ has done and what Christ is doing, only then does Paul call Timothy to do: "Follow the pattern of the sound words that you have heard from me, in the faith and love that are in Christ Jesus. By the Holy Spirit who dwells within us, guard the good deposit entrusted to you" (1:13–14). Timothy is to "follow" and to "guard," but even these activities are fueled by God's activity (1:13–14).

Our doing is only done by God's doing.

"Are there any examples of Christians who have done this?"
Here's one.

Remember What Others Did 1:16–18

Although many in Asia had turned away from Paul because of shame (1:15), and Timothy might have been tempted to do the same, Onesiphorus had done the opposite: "He often refreshed me and was not ashamed of my chains, but when he arrived in Rome he searched for me earnestly and found me—may the Lord grant him to find mercy from the Lord on that day!—and you well know all the service he rendered at Ephesus" (1:16–18). Onesiphorus was an example to Timothy of how to be unashamed of the gospel and those who suffer for it.

Self-encourage with others' courage.

> ### Changing Our Story with God's Story
>
> Because of Jesus's unashamed gospel work, we can work for the gospel without shame, as many others have done throughout the world and throughout the years.
>
> **Summary:** How can we stop being ashamed of the gospel? *Start with God's gospel work to restart your gospel work.*
>
> **Question:** How is the devil using gospel suffering to shame you into gospel silence?
>
> **Prayer:** Shameless God, you were not and are not ashamed of me. Therefore, use your gospel work to restart my own work by your grace.

More grace means more grit.

 Hear God's Story | Change Your Story | Tell the Story | Change Others' Stories

32

Sustainable and Affordable Energy

2 TIMOTHY 2:1-7

Fossil fuels, green energy, or nuclear power? The debates continue to rage over how to find sustainable and affordable energy for our planet's needs. Each of the proposed energy sources have pros and cons. Some are not sustainable enough, some are not affordable enough, and some are not powerful enough.

That debate will continue, but what's not debatable is the best source of sustainable and affordable spiritual energy—grace. Grace is God's saving love for those who deserve God's eternal anger.

How does grace energize us? In 2 Timothy 2:1-7, Paul challenges Timothy to be "strengthened by the grace that is in Christ Jesus" (2:1). If Timothy plugs into grace, he will see four powerful results which Paul presents with four powerful images.

Grace Strengthens Us to Multiply Like a Teacher 2:1-2

As he experienced the sovereign and steadfast love of Christ's grace, Timothy would find energy surging through him. Instead of cowering in silence and thinking only of surviving the moment, grace would enable Timothy to teach and train for the long term: "And what you have heard from me in the presence of many witnesses entrust to faithful men, who will be able to teach others also" (2:2). Paul taught Timothy, who would then teach faithful men, who would then teach others. By opening his mouth and teaching teachers, Timothy would multiply himself and the gospel for years to come.

Teachers teach teachers.

"But I'm not in a classroom. I'm on a battlefield."
Grace helps there too.

Grace Strengthens Us to Suffer Like a Soldier 2:3–4

As Timothy experienced the gracious love of Christ toward him, he would be willing and able to "share in suffering as a good soldier of Christ Jesus" (2:3). He would also resist the temptation to be half-in and half-out of the battle: "No soldier gets entangled in civilian pursuits, since his aim is to please the one who enlisted him" (2:4). Most soldiers fight out of love for their country, but Christian soldiers fight because they've been loved by their leader and they love to please him.

More grace means more grit.

"But sometimes it feels like I'm running a marathon."
Grace will get you to the end.

Grace Strengthens Us to Compete Like an Athlete 2:5

Paul wanted Timothy to win his spiritual race, but to do so he had to follow the rules: "An athlete is not crowned unless he competes according to the rules" (2:5). Timothy would not win any spiritual medals if he walked away from the course Christ set before him and simply ran his own race. Christ had set Timothy's course, and Christ's grace would enable him to run it no matter how many obstacles in it.

Grace runs with Christ, not away from Christ.

"Sometimes I wonder if I can keep going."
Grace gets you going and keeps you going.

Grace Strengthens Us to Work Hard Like a Farmer 2:6–7

By telling Timothy that "it is the hard-working farmer who ought to have the first share of the crops" (2:6), Paul encourages Timothy to work hard by grace so that he will share in the fruit of the gospel. Though grace is free and therefore the most affordable of all energy resources, God rewards those who depend upon grace in their service of him by multiplying grace in the lives of others. Working by grace produces the fruit of grace, which sustains the farmer by grace.

Great grace gives great grit.

Changing Our Story with God's Story

How do we get more of this powerful grace? We first need to think upon it more. As Paul wrote, "Think over what I say, for the Lord will give you understanding in everything" (2:7). As we think about grace, we will get wider, deeper, and longer grace.

Summary: How does grace energize us? *Plug into God's free love for the unlovable to teach, run, fight, and farm with sustainable and powerful energy.*

Question: What's your power source, and how can you increase your dependence on grace?

Prayer: God of all Grace, empty me of my own unaffordable, unsustainable, and ineffective strength, and fill me up with your free, forever, and forceful grace.

The boundless gospel will abound.

 Hear God's Story | Change Your Story | Tell the Story | Change Others' Stories

33

Three Therapeutic Thoughts

2 TIMOTHY 2:8–13

Our thoughts can make us ill. When we think of certain people, events, or experiences, we can make ourselves sick with stress. But equally, our thoughts can make us well. We can think of certain people, events, or experiences that calm us, cheer us, and relax us. Knowing this, *what thoughts can be therapeutic?*

Paul gives Timothy three thoughts to restore his health when suffering for the gospel. The first is the gospel itself, the second is the success of the gospel despite opposition, and the third is God's gospel faithfulness.

I Am Bound for the Gospel 2:8–9

Paul began with gospel therapy: "Remember Jesus Christ, risen from the dead, the offspring of David, as preached in my gospel, for which I am suffering, bound with chains as a criminal" (2:8–9). Yes, Paul says, I am bound for the gospel, but I remember the gospel I am bound for. It's the gospel of Jesus Christ who rose from the dead, the promised Son of David. That's what I'm bound for. It's worth being bound for this person, these deeds, these facts, and that message.

Painful gospel suffering is cured with truthful gospel facts.

"But won't the gospel fail if the best preachers are in prison?"
No, *because the gospel cannot be bound.*

The Gospel Is Not Bound 2:9–10

Paul says that though he is bound for the word of God, "the word of God is not bound!" (2:9). In other words, they can imprison us, but they cannot imprison the gospel. The result of this thought? "Therefore I endure everything for the sake of the elect, that they also may obtain the salvation that is in Christ Jesus with eternal glory" (2:10).

Paul wants Timothy to think about how gospel sufferings are worth it because the gospel continues to be blessed to the salvation of many, in time and for eternity. "Timothy, they can bind us, but they cannot bind the gospel. We may not be successful, but the gospel will be. We may be bound, but the gospel will never be bound."

The boundless gospel will abound.

"Why can the gospel not be bound?"
Because the Lord is bound to the gospel.

The Lord Is Bound to the Gospel 2:11–13

The third therapeutic thought is that the Lord binds himself to his word. This means God will keep his gospel promises. "The saying is trustworthy, for: If we have died with him, we will also live with him; if we endure, we will also reign with him" (2:11–12). If you die for him, you will live forever with him. If you suffer for him, you will sit on his throne with him.

But the Lord is also bound to his gospel threats. "If we deny him, he also will deny us; if we are faithless, he remains faithful—for he cannot deny himself" (2:12–13). God motivates not just with promises of reward for the faithful but guarantees of punishment for the unfaithful. The Lord cannot keep some of his word. He must keep all of it, both the promises and the warnings. Like Timothy, we must remind ourselves that God has bound himself to his word—his whole word.

God has bound himself to be himself.

Changing Our Story with God's Story

Jesus needed gospel therapy in his human nature. When he was intimidated, threatened, and abused, he reminded himself of gospel truth, the gospel's success, and his Father's gospel faithfulness. He received gospel therapy for his gospel pains. What a help to know that our divine therapist has also had therapy.

Summary: What thoughts can be therapeutic? *Think on God's gospel truth, God's gospel success, and God's gospel faithfulness for mental and spiritual health.*

Question: Which of these three thoughts provide the most therapy for you?

Prayer: Faithful God, bring gospel therapy deep into my soul for healthy holiness.

Work in the word, and the word will work.

 Hear God's Story | Change Your Story | Tell the Story | Change Others' Stories

34

Our Fatal Attraction

2 TIMOTHY 2:14–19

We have a fatal attraction to damaging and destructive words. That's why the most controversial and provocative people have the largest followings on social media. There's something about destructive words that draws us despite the damage they do to us. *How do we fix our fatal attraction to words that wound us?*

Long before the era of social media dawned, the apostle Paul saw the same dangers playing out in the ancient world that play out today in our online world. In 2 Timothy 2:14–19, Paul therefore not only issues a warning through Timothy about the destructive power of words but also sets out a positive plan to replace bad words with God's word. He begins by calling Timothy to shun quarreling words and irreverent words.

Avoid Bad Words 2:14, 17–18

Quarreling words ruin. "Remind them of these things, and charge them before God not to quarrel about words, which does no good, but only ruins the hearers" (2:14). Paul sees a huge difference between fighting for the truth and fighting over the truth. Fighting *for* the truth was about the truth winning. Fighting *about* the truth was about the fighters winning. Word wars start world wars.

Irreverent words infect. "Avoid irreverent babble, for it will lead people into more and more ungodliness, and their talk will spread like gangrene" (2:16–17). The quarrelers treat small words too importantly; the irreverent treat heavy words too lightly. Fighters were causing massive and obvious damage; laughers were causing equal damage but not so obviously. Irreverent diminishing of truth is more like a slow-spreading infection. A prime example of this is "Hymenaeus and Philetus, who have swerved from the truth, saying that the resurrection has already happened. They are upsetting the faith of some" (2:17–18).

Sticks and stones can break my bones, but words can break my soul.

"What words can stop the wars and cure the diseases?"
Only God's word can do that.

Work with God's Word 2:15, 19

God's revealed word is your workshop. "Do your best to present yourself to God as one approved, a worker who has no need to be ashamed, rightly handling the word of truth" (2:15). We all crave approval from our bosses; we want to work in such a way that our boss is happy to have hired us. For Timothy to enjoy God's approval, he is to work hard with God's word. Studying it and communicating it to others will take all his time and talents. It will be sore and sweaty work, but it will be worth the effort to have God smile proudly on him.

God's sealed word is your foundation. Working in the word will keep Timothy from futile fights and profane people. Remembering God's strong promises to his people will stabilize and strengthen him: "But God's firm foundation stands, bearing this seal: 'The Lord knows those who are his,' and, 'Let everyone who names the name of the Lord depart from iniquity'" (2:19). Paul warns Timothy about sinful human words but encourages him with God's holy words.

Work in the word, and the word will work.

Changing Our Story with God's Story

I'm constantly puzzled by my fatal attraction to killer words when God's life-giving word is right there and ready to do its healing and assuring work, if only I would put in the study work. And that's the problem right there, isn't it? Twitter is easier than the truth. Twitter doesn't need much work, but the truth heals and assures only when we put in the mental and spiritual effort. How much we need the work of the word in our lives if we are to put our work into the word.

Summary: How do we fix our fatal attraction to words that harm us? *Avoid bad words by working with God's word, and you'll build and not destroy, cure and not infect.*

Question: How can you deepen your sense of God's approval?

Prayer: Heavenly Employer, I crave your approval and therefore ask you to help me make good media choices that will build and not destroy, cure and not infect.

When Christians win, non-Christians win.

 Hear God's Story | Change Your Story | Tell the Story | Change Others' Stories

35

Spiritual Olympics

2 TIMOTHY 2:20-26

Competition improves us. That's why athletic records are often set at the Olympics; the international games bring together the world's top competitors every four years. Knowing this, the competitors train harder, better, and longer. The competitive spirit pushes them to grow, develop, and improve.

In 2 Timothy 2:20–26, the apostle Paul motivates Timothy with the competition he is facing. Paul wants his young protégé to adopt a competitive spirit in his Christian life and witness in order to improve his Christian life and witness. *How can competition improve our Christianity?*

Spiritual Competition Improves Self-Discipline 2:20–21

Athletes need self-discipline to succeed. They need to deny themselves many pleasures and submit to many pains if they are to win any medals. They may have a trainer to help them at points, but there are still many times when they are on their own and have to motivate themselves to get going and keep going.

Similarly, Timothy is to discipline his body, not for gold and silver honors but because he can become an honorable gold or silver vessel (2:20–21). Paul comes alongside Timothy as his trainer and uses vigorous athletic words to stir him up. "So flee youthful passions and pursue righteousness, faith, love, and peace (2:22). "Flee" and "pursue." It's not just "jog" and "look" but "sprint" and "chase." These are dynamic and forceful words that require maximum energy and effort.

World acclaim begins with solitary pain.

"I'm not sure I can do this on my own."
You don't have to.

Spiritual Competition Is Easier in a Team 2:22

Christianity is not a solo sport like golf but a team sport like football. Timothy was to flee and pursue "along with those who call on the Lord from a pure heart" (2:22). Solo Christianity is an oxymoron. It's like saying a "one-man team." Timothy is to discipline himself on his own, but he's also to compete alongside other Christians who seek the Lord and his holiness.

Christians are our teammates, not our competition.

"So, who is our competition?"
We win this competition when our competitors win.

Spiritual Competition Wants Everyone to Win 2:23–26

We don't win by using the same argumentative tactics as our opponents (2:23). Rather, "the Lord's servant must not be quarrelsome but kind to everyone, able to teach, patiently enduring evil, correcting his opponents with gentleness" (2:24–25). We beat our opponents not with better arguments but with better love. When they try to catch us out, twist our words, tie us in knots, and prove us wrong, we patiently and gently teach the truth. We focus not on winning the argument but on winning them. We don't try to beat them with force but win them with love. We compete, but we don't want there to be any losers.

Timothy was not to give up on any opponent because "God may perhaps grant them repentance leading to a knowledge of the truth, and they may come to their senses and escape from the snare of the devil, after being captured by him to do his will" (2:25–26). God may use our words to impart knowledge of what is true; that knowledge then brings them to sanity, and they are delivered from the devil's ensnaring ownership and power. Christians rejoice when their opponents win like this.

When Christians win, non-Christians win.

> ### Changing Our Story with God's Story
>
> We have a great team but an even better manager, Jesus Christ. He was the ultimate competitor who won multitudes with his muscular mercy. Now he works through his people as he disciples and trains them to compete so that everyone's a winner.
>
> **Summary:** How can competition improve our Christianity? *Compete with vigorous gentleness for great spiritual victories for all.*
>
> **Question:** How can you grow your gentleness muscle?
>
> **Prayer:** Victorious Lord, as you won me with your vigorous gentleness, help me to win others with vigorous gentleness.

Disordered love, disordered world.

 Hear God's Story | Change Your Story | Tell the Story | Change Others' Stories

36

Our Messed-Up World

2 TIMOTHY 3:1-9

How can we fix our messed-up world? That's the question that vexes and perplexes politicians every day. Many of them try their best to write laws and reorganize our society to fix things, but often end up only making things worse. That's because they don't understand the real cause of our problems. If they would read 2 Timothy 3:1-9, they would find the answer to what's wrong with our world—and discover that there's something wrong with them too.

Our Love Is Disordered 3:1-5

When God made us in his image, he made us with the ability to love. Our first parents Adam and Eve loved perfectly. They loved God with their whole heart, mind, soul, and strength, and they loved their neighbor as themselves. When they sinned, they disordered their love and the love of everyone descended from them. The results of that disordered love are seen everywhere in our dangerously disordered world.

Bad as things are, however, Paul warns Timothy that they are going to get even worse in the last days: "But understand this, that in the last days there will come times of difficulty" (3:1).

Love will become more disordered, making the world even more dangerous: "For people will be lovers of self, lovers of money . . . not loving good . . . lovers of pleasure rather than lovers of God"

(3:2-5). And the results? "People will be . . . proud, arrogant, abusive, disobedient to their parents, ungrateful, unholy, heartless, unappeasable, slanderous, without self-control, brutal . . . treacherous, reckless, swollen with conceit . . . having the appearance of godliness, but denying its power" (3:2-5). No wonder Paul warns Timothy, "Avoid such people" (3:5).

Disordered love, disordered world.

"But won't better education fix this?"
No, because our disordered love has disordered our minds as well.

Our Minds Are Disordered 3:6-9

Disordered love produces disordered minds. Instead of loving our neighbor as ourselves, we plot how to abuse our neighbors. In Timothy's day, that was seen in how some would "creep into households and capture weak women, burdened with sins and led astray by various passions" (3:6). Such disordered minds, both male and female, are "always learning and never able to arrive at a knowledge of the truth" (3:7). Indeed they "oppose the truth" and are "corrupted in mind" (3:8).

Although such disordered minds can do much damage, God sees their evil and will expose their evil in the future just as he did in the past. "Just as Jannes and Jambres opposed Moses, so these men also oppose the truth, men corrupted in mind and disqualified regarding the faith. But they will not get very far, for their folly will be plain to all, as was that of those two men" (3:8-9). God sees through them, and they will be seen for who they really are.

Clever devils face a more clever God.

Changing Our Story with God's Story

It's easy to look out at the world and see the danger of disordered love and disordered minds. But we also need to look at our inside world and confess that our loves and our minds are disordered and dangerous too. Yes, the world is dangerously disordered, but so is our internal world. Thankfully, if we are united to Christ, his Holy Spirit is at work reordering our loves and our minds. He's already brought a lot of order where there was previously chaos. But there's a lot more work to do, a work that will be completed only when we go to the perfectly ordered world of heaven.

Summary: How can we fix our messed-up world? *Look to the original Creator to reorder the world by reordering our loves and our minds.*

Question: Where do you see disorder in your own heart and mind? How is God reordering your loving and thinking?

Prayer: Creator of Order Out of Chaos, re-create our world order, starting with my chaos.

The all-sufficient Scriptures are an all-sufficient mentor.

 Hear God's Story | Change Your Story | Tell the Story | Change Others' Stories

37

Mentoring Matters

2 TIMOTHY 3:10-17

As mentoring has become an increasingly popular topic in Christian circles over recent years, I've had many young men ask if I would mentor them. While some of these relationships have been constructive and productive, many times the young men were just looking for a friendly chat about life over coffee. That's friendship, but it's not mentoring. *What then is mentoring?* In 2 Timothy 3:10–17, Paul gives us a model of Christian mentoring.

Christian Mentoring Aims at Growth in Grace 3:10

Mentoring is all about spiritual growth. It's concrete, specific, demanding, and challenging.

Look at how Paul specifies the nature of his mentoring relationship with Timothy: "You, however, have followed my teaching, my conduct, my aim in life, my faith, my patience, my love, my steadfastness" (3:10).

Paul had no qualms about confidently setting himself forth as a model and an example for Timothy to follow. As he did so, he demanded change and growth in Timothy's life in four main areas: his theology ("teaching"), his ethics ("conduct"), his purpose ("aim in life") and his spiritual character ("faith ... patience ... love ... steadfastness"). If they were in the same town, we can imagine they would have met and gone through this four-point checklist as Timothy was looking for progress in his spiritual life.

Mentoring is maturing.

"Spiritual growth, progress, and maturity sound great. Any downsides?"
Spiritual growth will always be opposed.

Christian Mentoring Results in Suffering for Grace 3:11–13

If Timothy grew in Paul-like theology, ethics, purpose, and character, he would also grow in Paul-like suffering. Growth in grace inevitably means growth in suffering. Paul did not hold back the reality of what growing Christians experience in a world that hates Christian growth. As Timothy followed Paul, he would follow his "persecutions and sufferings that happened to me at Antioch, at Iconium, and at Lystra—which persecutions I endured; yet from them all the Lord rescued me" (3:11).

And just in case Timothy thinks that he can manage to grow in grace without growing in suffering, Paul affirms, "Indeed, all who desire to live a godly life in Christ Jesus will be persecuted" (3:12). Bad as it's been for Paul, it's going to get worse for Timothy in the future: "Evil people and impostors will go on from bad to worse, deceiving and being deceived" (3:13).

A Christlike life brings Christlike suffering.

"If I rely on a mentor, what happens when he's no longer around?"
The word is our ever-present mentor.

Christian Mentoring Is Sustained by the Word of Grace 3:14–17

Paul won't always be around for Timothy. Paul will eventually be persecuted into prison and death. How then can Timothy continue to grow in grace and suffer for grace? Paul points him to the Scriptures for ongoing mentoring: "But as for you, continue in what you have learned and have firmly believed, knowing from whom you learned it and how from childhood you have been acquainted with the sacred writings, which are able to make you wise for salvation through faith in Christ Jesus" (3:14–15).

How is Scripture so powerful that it can continue to mentor Timothy even when Paul is absent? "All Scripture is breathed out by God and profitable for teaching, for reproof, for correction, and for training in righteousness, that the man of God may be complete, equipped for every good work" (3:16–17). Paul's mentoring was helpful to Timothy, but the Bible was vital. Mentoring was a beneficial option, but the Bible was a nonnegotiable. Paul could do a lot for Timothy, but the Bible can do even more as God powerfully mentors his people with it.

The all-sufficient Scriptures are an all-sufficient mentor.

Changing Our Story with God's Story

When someone asks me to mentor him, the first area I ask about is Bible reading. Unless someone is being mentored by God through his word, no amount of my mentoring can make any difference.

Summary: How can I get a mentor? *Start by getting mentored by God through the Bible for growth in grace and suffering.*

Question: How is God mentoring you with his word today?

Prayer: Ever-Present Mentor, grow me through your word so that I can make progress in Christlike grace and Christlike suffering.

Preach to needs, not to wants.

 Hear God's Story | Change Your Story | Tell the Story | Change Others' Stories

38

The Greatest Blessing Can Be the Worst Curse

2 TIMOTHY 4:1–5

One of the greatest blessings of the internet is how much access we now have to the best preachers and teachers. One of the worst curses of the internet is how much access we now have to the best preachers and teachers!

As some have warned over recent years, many Christians have become so used to the rich buffet of gifted preaching and teaching available to them at the tap of a finger or the click of a mouse that they have grown bored and dissatisfied with their own local church pastors. The ease of access, however, also exposes them to the dangers of false teachers and false teaching.

How do we respond to the challenges of podcast pastors and celebrity pastors? Although we might not expect the Bible to address such issues, God foresaw this age and inspired the apostle Paul to write 2 Timothy 4:1–5.

People Will Want Different Words 4:3–4

You'd think Paul was living in the twenty-first century when he wrote, "For the time is coming when people will not endure sound teaching, but having itching ears they will accumulate for themselves teachers to suit their own passions, and will turn away from listening to the truth and wander off into myths" (4:3–4). When ordinary truth no longer satisfies the heart, itching ears crave to be scratched with novelty. It's truly staggering how Christians can turn away from pastors who have proven themselves faithful for decades and turn to celebrity online entertainers and their latest eye-catching and ear-scratching fads.

Just as we can pick whatever we feel like eating at a buffet, we can pick whatever sermons we feel like hearing and "teachers to suit our own passions." How can basic meat and potatoes for the heart compete with the variety of spices and sugars that appeal to our flesh?

Itchy ears empty hearts.

What should we do when people turn away from the truth?

We Preach the Same Words 4:1, 4–5

Paul recognized the tendency in preachers and teachers to try to copy the latest popular preachers in matter and manner, and solemnly warned against this: "I charge you in the presence of God and of Christ Jesus, who is to judge the living and the dead, and by his appearing and his kingdom, preach the word; be ready in season and out of season; reprove, rebuke, and exhort, with complete patience and teaching" (4:1–2). When podcast pastors are giving people what they want, faithful pastors are to give people what they need. For motivation, Paul reminded Timothy that he ministered in the presence of God more than people, and that his work would be assessed by God more than by the culture.

Therefore, when people want political commentary, give them what they need—preach the word. When people want change, give them what they need—the same truth whatever the season. When they want humor, stories, and happy feelings, give them what they need—reproof, rebuke, and exhortation. When people want popular pastors, be what they need—a patient pastor. When people want entertainment, give them what they need—teaching.

Yes, so-called "celebrity pastors" seem to be always happy and prosperous, having lots of leisure time for sports and vacations. But "as for you, always be sober-minded, endure suffering, do the work of an evangelist, fulfill your ministry" (4:5).

Preach to needs, not to wants.

Changing Our Story with God's Story

Paul's description of a faithful pastor also fits the most faithful pastor of all time—Jesus Christ. When people wanted different human words; he preached the same divine words.

Summary: How do we navigate the challenges of podcast pastors and celebrity pastors? *When people want different words, give them the same word, and when people want a celebrity pastor, give them a serious pastor.*

Question: How can you use the internet in a way that does not undermine your faith or your pastor?

Prayer: God of Truth, thank you for telling me what I needed to hear rather than what I wanted to hear. Thank you for pastors who are truth-tellers rather than ear-scratchers.

When we're ready to die, we're ready to live.

 Hear God's Story | Change Your Story | Tell the Story | Change Others' Stories

39

It's Time to Go Home

2 TIMOTHY 4:6-8

Last words are lingering words. They leave a lasting impact on those who hear them. That's why Ray Robinson's book, *Famous Last Words: Fond Farewells, Deathbed Diatribes, and Exclamations upon Expiration*, has been widely read.[1] From John Maynard Keynes's "I wish I had drunk more champagne," to Thomas Edison's "It's very beautiful over there," people's last words reveal much about their character. So, if you had the choice, *what would your last words be?* We find some of Paul's last words in 2 Timothy 4:6–8.

I Am Ready to Go 4:6

"For I am already being poured out as a drink offering" (4:6). A drink offering was the final act of the sacrificial ceremony. When the animal had been butchered, bled, and burned, wine was poured upon it to complete the sacrifice. As Paul looked back at his life of sacrificial service (Rom. 12:1), he realized that his life was in its final phase.

"The time of my departure has come" (4:6). Having departed from multiple harbors in his many missionary endeavors, Paul was making arrangements for his final departure of his final journey, not just from a harbor but from this earth.

---

1   Ray Robinson, *Famous Last Words: Fond Farewells, Deathbed Diatribes, and Exclamations upon Expiration* (NY: Workman, 2003).

As Paul reflected on the end of his earthly life, there's not a hint of resentful rebellion, but only glad submission. He knew the end was near, and he was ready to go. With the last drops of the drink offering dripping out and the last ropes being cast off from the dock, his attitude was "Let's do this."

When we're ready to die, we're ready to live.

"What do I do in the meantime?"
Complete your work.

I've Completed My Work 4:7

Paul summed up his work as a fighter, a runner, and a guard. Paul was a *fighter*. "I have fought the good fight" (4:7). Paul fought for the truth and against all enemies of it. Using the weapons of God's word and prayer, he fought for the faith and against unbelief. It was a holy and just war that brought much spiritual good to Paul and the world.

Paul was a *runner*. "I have finished the race" (4:7). God designs different courses for different Christians. Paul was now on the finishing straight of the last lap of his unique race and was just a few steps from the finish line. He could therefore look back with relief and satisfaction that he had run the race God set out for him.

Paul was a *guard*. "I have kept the faith" (4:7). "The faith" could mean Paul's own personal trust in the Savior, but he's more likely referring to the truths of the Christian faith, "the faith that was once for all delivered to the saints" (Jude 3). Paul had jealously guarded and conserved this precious deposit of truth, refusing to give up one letter of it in any circumstances.

Fight for the faith, run the race of faith,
and guard the faith, for a satisfying faith.

"Will it be worth it?"
Look at your head.

I Will Be Crowned 4:8

Fighting, running, and guarding are demanding callings. If Paul only looked backward, all he would see were wounds and scars. That's why he looked forward to the reward every fighter, every runner, and every guard will receive: "Henceforth there is laid up for me the crown of righteousness, which the Lord, the righteous judge, will award to me on that day, and not only to me but also to all who have loved his appearing" (4:8).

Look ahead to your head.

Changing Our Story with God's Story

Paul did not have sinless submission, sinless satisfaction, or sinless anticipation. But Jesus did. He could say these words in a way no other could. His sinless life and death atone for our sinful lives and deaths.

Summary: What would your last words be? *Live so that you can die with submission, satisfaction, and anticipation.*

Question: If you were to write out your last words, what would they be?

Prayer: Lord of Life and Death, help me to live so that I can die with submission, satisfaction, and anticipation.

God gives us appointments with disappointments.

 Hear God's Story | Change Your Story | Tell the Story | Change Others' Stories

40

God Appoints Our Disappointments

2 TIMOTHY 4:10-22

Christians let us down and get us down. How many times we've had certain expectations of others, and they did the unexpected. They said one thing and did another. We trusted them, and they broke that trust. It's depressing and even infuriating, isn't it? We get down and angry with them, with ourselves, and even with God. *How should we respond when people disappoint us?*

The apostle Paul certainly had his share of people-disappointments. He had so many betrayals, letdowns, and setbacks; it's amazing he didn't just give up in cynical discouragement. In 2 Timothy 4:10–22, we observe how God led him through these relational busts.

Some People Are Disappointing 4:10, 14–16

Paul does not deny his people-disappointments. He faces them, feels the pain of them, and learns from them. He gives us three examples of this. First, he tells us that "Demas, in love with this present world, has deserted me and gone to Thessalonica" (4:10). A colaborer abandoned eternal work for this present world.

Second, Paul is disappointed not just by abandonment but by hostile opposition. "Alexander the coppersmith did me great harm; the Lord will repay him according to his deeds. Beware of him yourself, for he strongly opposed our message" (4:14–15). Paul gives justice into God's hands but also wants the church to avoid experiencing his pain.

Third, Paul is disappointed by absence. Demas left him, Alexander opposed him, and others simply didn't show up. "At my first defense no one came to stand by me, but all deserted me. May it not be charged against them!" (4:16). Paul turned up for his day in court, but none of his friends did.

God gives us appointments with disappointments.

"Do we just give up on people then?"
No, because God's grace can bring them back.

Some People Are Redeemable 4:11

Mark had been a disappointment to Paul in the past, having proven an unreliable missionary partner (Acts 13:13; 15:36–39). But now, years later, God has redeemed this relationship to such an extent that Paul says, "Get Mark and bring him with you, for he is very useful to me for ministry" (4:11). Mark is now a boost to Paul, not a bust.

Our letdowns can become liftoffs.

"How do we avoid cynicism in the meantime?"
By remembering those who never disappointed us.

Some People Are Helpful 4:10–12, 19–21

Paul didn't focus on the negatives. Rather, when negatives invaded his mind, he expelled them with positives. He lists a number of people who were his encouragers and helpers in gospel work: Crescens, Titus, Luke, Tychicus, Timothy, Prisca and Aquila, Onesiphorus's family, Erastus, Eubulus, Pudens, Linus, Claudia, and many other brothers (4:10–12, 19–21). Paul did not let his disappointments blind him to real and reliable gospel friendships.

God helps us through helpers.

"What's our ultimate support in people-disappointments?"
The God who never disappoints.

The Lord Is Essential 4:17–18

Although Paul experienced a redeemed relationship with Mark and enjoyed reliable relationships with others, his ultimate confidence was in God not people. When everyone else left him, he reminds us that "the Lord stood by me and strengthened me, so that through me the message might be fully proclaimed and all the Gentiles might hear it. So I was rescued from the lion's mouth" (4:17).

The Lord's faithfulness amid much faithlessness gave him great faith for the future. "The Lord will rescue me from every evil deed and bring me safely into his heavenly kingdom. To him be the glory forever and ever. Amen" (4:18). What a perfect final flourish for his letters.

People are helpful, but the Lord is essential.

> ### Changing Our Story with God's Story
>
> Jesus had even more disappointments than Paul, but he also redeemed his disappointments, continued to make disciples who would disappoint him, and ultimately cast himself upon God alone in his loneliest and lowest disappointments.
>
> **Summary:** How should we respond when people disappoint us? *Cast yourself upon the God who never disappoints.*
>
> **Question:** How can you change your response to your most recent disappointment?
>
> **Prayer:** Faithful God, use human disappointments to decrease my faith in people and increase my faith in you.

TITUS

We hope for never-ending life in a world of never-ending death.

 Hear God's Story | Change Your Story | Tell the Story | Change Others' Stories

41

Hope in a Hopeless World

TITUS 1:1–4

Optimists have better health, better relationships, better careers, and less stress, and they even live eight to ten years longer than average.[1] Yet many of us struggle to have an optimistic outlook. When we see the deterioration of our culture, we fear the worst rather than hope for the best. *How can we become more optimistic?*

The apostle Paul's culture was no better than our own. Yet, although he was pessimistic on a societal level, he was optimistic at the personal level, as we see in his letter to the young Pastor Titus who was struggling to hope in a hopeless time.

Our Hope Is Eternal Life 1:1–2

Paul opens his letter by reminding Titus of his own divine calling: "Paul, a servant of God and an apostle of Jesus Christ, for the sake of the faith of God's elect and their knowledge of the truth, which accords with godliness, in hope of eternal life" (1:1). He was no ordinary religious teacher, but rather was a servant of God and an apostle of Christ sent to help God's people grow in faith, knowledge, and hope.

---

[1] See "The Benefits of Being Optimistic," on the Are You Optimistic or Pessimistic? website, https://www.seemypersonality.com/Optimism-Test#q1; and "Optimism Lengthens Life Study Finds," *The Harvard Gazette*, https://news.harvard.edu/gazette/.

Faith leads to knowledge, which leads to hope. But it's a very specific kind of hope. It's not hope that the world will become a better place, or that people in general will become a better people. No, this hope is personal, eternal, and heavenly. Paul looks ahead, beyond this world and beyond time, to a far better world and time.

We hope for never-ending life in
a world of never-ending death.

"How can I be sure this hope is real?"
Look to the God who promised it.

God Promised Eternal Life 1:2

How can we have sure hope of eternal life? The prospect of eternal life is founded on the promises of the eternal "God, who never lies," and who promised this eternal life "before the ages began" (1:2).

Many optimists cannot explain the basis of their hope for a better future. Others might base their hope on education or technology. How strong is such hope? How secure?

Even if some secure hope could be discovered that would guarantee a better future for our world, what about after that? What hope is there for life after death? If people think about this at all, they usually base their hopes on their own efforts and works. But how strong is such hope? How secure?

The hope Paul instills in Titus is strong and secure because it is based on the promises of the God who never lies. This is no religious huckster making empty and deceitful promises. This is the God who keeps every promise he has ever made.

The truthfulness of the promisor
is the truth of the promise.

"I need this promise. Where can I find out more?"
In the preaching of salvation.

Preaching Reveals Eternal Life 1:3-4

These divine promises of eternal life can be found throughout the Old Testament. But when will all these promises be fulfilled? Paul tells Timothy that they already have been. They were "at the proper time manifested in his word through the preaching with which I have been entrusted by the command of God our Savior" (1:3).

Multiple seed promises in the Old Testament came to full bloom in the coming of Christ who lived, suffered, died, and rose again. Now, by preaching, the petals of that most beautiful flower are revealed to all to attract all and fill all with hope.

That's why Titus, Paul's "true child in a common faith," and every other believer can enjoy "grace and peace from God the Father and Christ Jesus our Savior" (1:4).

Grace and peace lead to hope and optimism.

> ### Changing Our Story with God's Story
>
> In the next chapter, Paul will herald Christ as our blessed hope (2:13). No hope is as happy as hope in Christ.
>
> **Summary:** How can we become more optimistic? *Nurture optimism by nurturing the true hope of eternal life.*
>
> **Question:** How can you nurture the hope of eternal life?
>
> **Prayer:** Eternal God, grow my hope of eternal life in a world of true pessimism and false optimism.

God's word is the world's hope.

 Hear God's Story | Change Your Story | Tell the Story | Change Others' Stories

42

Authority Authors Hope

TITUS 1:5-9

"Why do I need elders? Who gave them authority over me? Why should I listen to them?" The anti-authority spirit of our age has entered the church, with many resenting and rejecting the oversight of elders and being accountable to them. This not only undermines good order in the church but also undermines hope in the lives of such spiritual rebels.

"How can you say that the loss of spiritual hope is connected to the loss of spiritual authority?"

Because that's what Paul says. In Titus 1, after speaking of spiritual hope (1:1–4), he immediately speaks of the importance of installing elders. Paul explained the hope of eternal life that God promised in the Old Testament and revealed in the New Testament and then writes, "This is why I left you in Crete, so that you might put what remained into order, and appoint elders in every town as I directed you" (1:5). *How do elders help us increase hope?*

Elders Nurture Hope by Their Lives 1:6-8

Hope changes our character and conduct (1 John 3:3). Our character and conduct therefore reflect our hope. So what kind of character and conduct would reflect an elder's hope of eternal life through Christ?

Twice, Paul says an elder must be "above reproach" (1:6–7), meaning that no allegation or accusation would stick to him. How does that come about? By being a faithful husband in marriage, a faithful father in his family, a faithful member of his community, a faithful citizen, and a faithful employee (1:6). If he is faithful in these areas, he will be a faithful steward and overseer in God's family (1:7).

Elders lack every vice and possess every virtue. They "must not be arrogant or quick-tempered or a drunkard or violent or greedy for gain" (1:7). Rather, they will be "hospitable, a lover of good, self-controlled, upright, holy, and disciplined" (1:8).

As the stories behind mass shooters often reveal, when people lose hope, their character and conduct reflect that despair. However, elders prove, demonstrate, and encourage hope by their godly lives. Nothing can explain their character or conduct but their spiritual hope.

Hopeful believers are holy people.

"So, elders just need to be good and do good?"
No, they also have to speak good.

Elders Nurture Hope with Their Teaching 1:9

As people are attracted to elders by their godly lives, they will want to know a reason for the hope that is in them (1 Pet. 3:15). When asked, "Why are you hopeful?" the elder "must hold firm to the trustworthy word as taught, so that he may be able to give instruction in sound doctrine and also to rebuke those who contradict it" (1:9).

As elders read and explain the Bible, it is inevitable that the reason for their hope will be given. But they must not only teach the word and instruct in doctrine; they must also firmly admonish any who oppose God's word. Hope is too important to be left defenseless in the face of critical pessimists.

God's word is the world's hope.

Changing Our Story with God's Story

We cannot expect perfection from our elders. To the extent that they live faithful lives and speak with godly lips, we will grow in optimistic hope. But they often fail. That doesn't mean we turn away from these imperfect men. No, we continue to use them as a resource, but we also see them pointing us to the perfect older overseer, Jesus Christ, whose faithful life and godly lips kindle hope in us more than any other can.

Summary: Why do we need elders? *Use godly elders to nurture hope through their faithful lives and truthful lips.*

Question: How can you utilize your elders to grow your hope?

Prayer: God of Hope, grow hope in me through the faithful lives and truthful lips of godly elders.

Without faith in the only one who is good, we cannot do one good thing.

 Hear God's Story | Change Your Story | Tell the Story | Change Others' Stories

43

Facing False Teachers

TITUS 1:10–16

What would you rather do: give hope or fight a war? Offer comfort to others or suffer discomfort yourself? Revive believers or rebuke unbelievers? Most of us (I hope!) would prefer the former to the latter in these pairs of choices. However, elders are to do both. Spiritual leaders are tasked with not only with giving hope to believers but also rebuking false teachers.

Titus was facing unbelieving opponents who were a mortal threat to the believers he was shepherding. With wolves at the door of the sheepfold, Paul called Timothy to go to battle with them for the good of the sheep. *How are false teachers to be dealt with?*

Silence Empty Talkers 1:10–11

Although some today think that it's "unchristian" or "unloving" to critique and condemn false teachers, Paul insisted that it was both Christian and loving. Why? "They are upsetting whole families by teaching for shameful gain what they ought not to teach" (1:11). Paul saw the damage they were doing to precious souls, and that their aim was not the profit of others but their own profit.

That's why he had no hesitation in calling them "insubordinate, empty talkers and deceivers" (1:10). They were spiritual rebels, spiritual vacuums, and spiritual actors. They came from many different backgrounds, but the worst were "those of the circumcision party" (1:10). These were false teachers who plagued Paul wherever he went, teaching that the Old Testament law still had to be kept for salvation. Such dangerous and damning doctrine must be defeated for the good of souls.

Empty talkers can make a lot of noise.

"Why are false teachers so dangerous?"
Because they target our unique weaknesses.

Beware of Cultural Weaknesses 1:12–14

Each culture has its strengths and weaknesses. Some of this is historical, some of it is genetic, and some of it is modeling. Although it's not considered polite today, Paul did not hesitate to point out the cultural weaknesses of different cultures, because that was where the devil often attacked.

Try to imagine the Cretan believers as Titus shared Paul's letter to them: "One of the Cretans, a prophet of their own, said, 'Cretans are always liars, evil beasts, lazy gluttons.' This testimony is true. Therefore rebuke them sharply, that they may be sound in the faith, not devoting themselves to Jewish myths and the commands of people who turn away from the truth" (1:12–14). Paul quoted Epimedes, a famous Cretan poet, and agreed with his analysis of the Cretan character weakness. Titus was instructed to pass this on as a rebuke of their cultural weakness to believe and communicate lies, to be lazy in thinking, and to easily be deceived by various myths and falsehoods.

These false teachers tried to reinstate Old Testament laws about external purification, not realizing that they were defiled in their hearts and minds and therefore impure before God no matter how careful they were about external cleanliness (1:15).

In one final flourish Paul puts the stamp of God's execration upon them: "They profess to know God, but they deny him by their works. They are detestable, disobedient, unfit for any good work" (1:16). No matter how hard they worked to do good and be good, without faith in Christ, they were detestable to God and completely unable to perform any good.

Without faith in the only one who is good,
we cannot do one good thing.

Changing Our Story with God's Story

Jesus modeled how to be both the most loving evangelist of the lost and the fiercest rebuker of false teaching. He reserved his greatest anger for the wolves of his day because he reserved his greatest love for his sheep for eternity.

Summary: How are false teachers to be dealt with? *Recognize that false teachers will target cultural weaknesses, and reject them as firmly as Paul did.*

Question: How would false teachers take advantage of your own weakness? Your church's weakness? Your culture's weakness?

Prayer: God of Truth, enable me not only to believe all truth but to reject all lies and rebuke all liars for my own good and the good of others.

Selfishness takes no work, but selflessness is the hardest work.

 Hear God's Story | Change Your Story | Tell the Story | Change Others' Stories

44

Sound Doctrine and Sound Life

TITUS 2:1–6

Christian A: "I'm not very theological. I'm more of a practical Christian."
Christian B: "Sound doctrine is far more important than good morals."
Paul: "Sound doctrine and a sound life are inseparable."

The apostle Paul instructed Titus, "But as for you, teach what accords with sound [that is, "true and substantial"] doctrine" (2:1). Titus was to teach doctrine and morals, theology and practice because sound doctrine produces a sound life, and a sound life reveals sound doctrine.

What does a sound life look like? While there are ethical practices common to all Christians, in Titus 2:1–6, Paul spotlighted age-specific and sex-specific ethical problems and practices for different demographics.

Older Men Are to Be Serious 2:2

Many men, as they age, lose their spiritual edge. Having served the Lord with zeal in their youth, they begin to think of retirement and relaxation. As leisure and hobbies fill more and more of their time, they can drift in their doctrine, character, courage, and ethics.

That's why Titus is to teach the older men "to be sober-minded, dignified, self-controlled, sound in faith, in love, and in steadfastness" (2:2). Lives of leisure and pleasure are not conducive to spiritual seriousness, self-control, soundness, or steadfastness.

Senior spirituality is serious spirituality.

What about older women?
Paul has words tailored for them too.

Older Women Are to Be Supermodels 2:3–4

When older women slacken in their later years, they can lose control of their mouths, leading to irreverent words, slanderous gossip, and habitual drunkenness. This bad example filters down to the next generation of Christian women, leading them astray.

Hence, Titus is to exhort the older women to be "reverent in behavior, not slanderers or slaves to much wine. They are to teach what is good, and so train the young women" (2:3–4). They are to be supermodels of godliness and goodness and so provide a holy pattern for young women to follow.

Spiritual mothers are to be spiritual supermodels.

What about the younger generation?
Paul also has specific words for their specific sins.

Younger Women Are to Be Selfless 2:4–5

Selflessness does not come naturally to anyone. That's why Paul calls the older women to train the young women away from selfishness to selflessness: "Train the young women to love their husbands and children, to be self-controlled, pure, working at home, kind, and submissive to their own husbands, that the word of God may not be reviled" (2:4–5). This hard and rigorous training will redirect them from self-love to family love, from self-assertion to self-denial, from self-centeredness to God-centeredness, from self-promotion to God-promotion.

Selfishness takes no work, but selflessness is the hardest work.

"What about the young men?"
They are to be self-controlled.

Younger Men Are to Be Self-Controlled 2:6

"Likewise, urge the younger men to be self-controlled" (2:6). That's it? One command? Are young men not so sinful, compared to other demographics? Do young men not need to correct anything other than self-control?

Not at all. Remember, the whole letter is addressed to a young man. Also, Paul will give specific direction to Titus in the next verses. But perhaps Paul also sees that if young men could master this one area, it would change everything about them.

Self-control means God is in control.

Changing Our Story with God's Story

If we focus on doctrine but not duty, or duty instead of doctrine, we will lose both doctrine and duty. Gospel truth fuels gospel living, and gospel living is guided by gospel truth. Although different demographics have different ethical challenges, the gospel is enough to empower and direct change for all.

Ethical exhortations always point us to Jesus who, during his entire earthly life, gathered together all the scattered beauties of the saints. He was a serious supermodel, selfless and self-controlled at every stage of his life. He offers his righteousness in exchange for our unrighteousness.

Summary: What does a sound life look like? *Defeat specific sins with specific truths.*

Question: What specific temptation are you facing at this stage of your life, and what truth can help you overcome it?

Prayer: Good God, empower good living with your good truth so that I can be a motivator and model of good for my generation.

Show off to others what God has showed to you.

 Hear God's Story | Change Your Story | Tell the Story | Change Others' Stories

45

A Good Show-Off

TITUS 2:7–8

God loves show-offs. Not the kind that live to show how good they are but those who live to show how good God is. They show God off rather than show themselves off. Pastors are to be especially good at this kind of showing off. They are not to hide God's work and God's word but are to show it, to exhibit it, and to model it for others to see.

So should nonpastors just skip this chapter? Not at all, because all Christians, not just pastors, are called to show off, to some degree. Also, pastors need people to show off to. Therefore, Titus 2:7 doesn't call us simply to be show off but to see show-offs and copy them. *How can we be better show-offs for God?*

Show Off God's Good Work and Word 2:7–8

We are to show off God's good work in us. "Show yourself in all respects to be a model of good works" (2:7). When people looked at Titus, they were to see an example, a pattern, of moral ethics and practical works. Titus was to live in a way that demonstrated what the Christian life looked like and also induced them to live it.

We are to show off God's good word from us. "And in your teaching show integrity, dignity, and sound speech that cannot be condemned" (2:7–8). Showing "integrity" meant demonstrating consistency in Titus's teaching, not contradiction or confusion. Teaching with "dignity" meant a manner of speaking that suited the weight and seriousness of the words. He was an ambassador not a comedian. "Sound speech that cannot be condemned" meant teaching the truth so clearly and accurately that no one could find fault with it

This kind of showing off would have an impact on Christians as well as non-Christians: "So that an opponent may be put to shame, having nothing evil to say about us" (2:8). By modeling God's good work and word, not only would Christians be inspired and instructed, but non-Christians would be shamed and silenced.

Show off to others what God has showed to you.

"But I'm not a pastor."
You can still see even if you can't show.

See God's Good Work and Word 2:7–8

There's no show without spectators. By calling Titus to show, God was also calling those around him to see. Titus was to show, and the people were to see. As the people read and heard this letter to Titus, they would realize that it involved them too.

See God's good work in your pastor. Use your pastor as a model of what it means to be a Christian. As he shows, see what he is showing. Watch him, use him as a pattern, and copy his conduct.

Hear God's good word in your pastor. As your pastor shows integrity, dignity, and soundness in his teaching, rejoice in it rather than reject it. Repeat his good words in your family, among friends, and at work.

As you see and hear your pastor's show, you too will begin to show God's work and word, and both Christians and non-Christians will get spiritual benefit.

See the show to show and tell.

Changing Our Story with God's Story

Paul tried to be an example. Titus tried to be an example. And we try to be examples. But everyone inevitably fails. That doesn't mean we stop trying to do better; it does mean we start trusting in Christ better. He is the only stainless example in word and work, and we worship him as such. He fulfilled these verses stainlessly, and his stainless blood removed all our stains.

Summary: How can we be better show-offs? *Show off God's good works and God's good word so that others will see your show and want to start their own show.*

Question: What have you seen in your pastors that you need to show in your life?

Prayer: Good God, open my eyes to see your show-offs better and open my life so that others can see your show better.

Please your master to please the Master.

 Hear God's Story | Change Your Story | Tell the Story | Change Others' Stories

46

"I Hate My Boss"

TITUS 2:9–10

The jobsite Monster.com polled a thousand people who were actively seeking new jobs. The number one reason for wanting a change, chosen by 76 percent of respondents, was having a toxic boss. According to the survey, the most common marks of a toxic boss included being power-hungry, self-seeking, micromanaging, incompetent, or simply not available.[1] With 65 percent of American workers actively seeking a new job at the time of writing, there must be a lot of toxic bosses around.[2]

In the apostle Paul's day many of the early Christians were slaves who could not switch jobs whenever they wanted. While recognizing the injustice of slavery, the apostle wanted to help Christian slaves honor God in this painful calling. Therefore, in Titus 2:9–10, he gave instruction about how to be Christian slaves. *What can twenty-first century workers learn from first-century slaves?*

Submit to Your Masters 2:9

What was the last word unhappy slaves wanted to hear? *Submit.* Yet Paul said this was their duty: "Bondservants are to be submissive to their own masters in everything" (2:9). They were to submit not just in the easy things or in the big things, but in everything (unless, of course, it contradicted God's law).

---

1 Gene Marks, "Monster Poll: 76 Percent of Jobseekers Say Their Boss Is Toxic," *Inc.*, https://www.inc.com/.
2 Megan Leonhardt, "Job-Hopping Heats Up: 65% of U.S. Workers Are Looking for a New Job," *Fortune*, August 20, 2021, https://fortune.com.

Submit meant "obey," not just in word, but in action; and not just in action, but in heart. Slaves were to respectfully follow their master's instructions.

Submit to your master to please the Master.

"That's going to be really tough. Is that it?"
No, it's going to be even harder.

Please Your Masters 2:9–10

Paul didn't stop at *submitting* to masters; he pushed the slaves to also *please* their masters. They were "to be well-pleasing" (2:9). Not only were they to submit with a smile on their face; they were to work to put a smile on their master's face. That meant going beyond mere duty to actively finding ways to make their master happy. Some specific examples follow: "Not argumentative, not pilfering, but showing all good faith." Agree instead of argue, give instead of take, and be trustworthy rather than suspect.

Please your master to please the Master.

"OK, submit and please. That's it now, right?"
No. The hardest of all is next.

Witness to Your Masters 2:10

What could be harder than a slave having to submit to a bad boss and even please a bad boss? Seeking the salvation of a bad boss. Submitting and pleasing is all about soul-winning: "So that in everything they may adorn the doctrine of God our Savior" (2:10).

By submitting to their masters and pleasing their masters, they would be different from all the other slaves. While unbelieving slaves wore the ugly clothes of rebellion and resentment, believing slaves were to wear the beautiful robes of joyful service. This kind of character and conduct would embody the truth of the gospel; it would give living form to "the doctrine of God our Savior." It would present the character and conduct of our Savior's self-denying service for the good of others and so be a means of attracting their masters to the Savior.

Witness to your master to witness for your Master.

Changing Our Story with God's Story

No matter how bad we think our boss is, the slaves' bosses were worse. So, if God through Paul expected them to submit to, please, and witness to their bosses, how much more does he expect us to do the same?

This does not mean that we can never leave our boss, but it does mean that having a bad boss is a great opportunity to show a good Savior. It shows our earthly boss that we have a heavenly boss, which makes us a different kind of worker than everyone else.

Summary: What can twenty-first-century workers learn from first-century slaves? *Wear the attractive clothes of submission and obedience to please your master and win him for Christ.*

Question: How can you put this into practice in your workplace?

Prayer: My Good Master, I have a bad master. Please give me the ability to obey him and please him so that I might win him for you.

Grace costs nothing but demands everything.

 Hear God's Story | Change Your Story | Tell the Story | Change Others' Stories

47

Do You Have a Trainer?

TITUS 2:11–14

I've tried many ways to build regular exercise into my life, and most of them have petered out after a few weeks or months. The only time I enjoyed a lengthy period of consistent daily exercise was when I hired a personal trainer. That motivated me because it put a nonnegotiable daily appointment in my calendar; I knew that for once I was doing appropriate exercises the right way; I felt and saw the progress in my body; and, most of all, I was paying for the trainer's expertise and therefore didn't want to waste my money.

If we are to be consistent in regular and helpful spiritual exercise, we need a trainer to guide us, motivate us, and keep us accountable. *How can we get a spiritual trainer?* In Titus 2:11–14, Paul introduces us to the best spiritual trainer—grace.

Grace Saves Us 2:11

Before grace trains us, grace must save us: "For the grace of God has appeared, bringing salvation for all people" (2:11). We do not train our way to salvation, but rather trust our way to salvation.

When did the grace of God appear? Although God's grace was vaguely visible in the Old Testament, the curtain was pulled back and the spotlight turned on in the New Testament when Christ came. When he appeared on earth, salvation appeared to the world. The light of his undeserved love flooded the earth as the gospel was carried to the ends of the earth.

Our grit doesn't save, but God's grace does.

"Am I finished with grace when I get saved by grace?"
No, grace is just getting started.

Grace Trains Us 2:12-14

Once grace has saved us, it begins to train us. Grace gets us enrolled in the gym for nothing, but then begins to get us into spiritual shape with a range of spiritual exercises.

Grace trains us to renounce sin. "Training us to renounce ungodliness and worldly passions" (2:12). This means rejecting and abandoning sin.

Grace trains us to be self-disciplined. "Training us . . . to live self-controlled, upright, and godly lives in the present age" (2:12). Before grace, we had little ability to resist temptation. But when God's undeserved love enters our system, it gives us new ability to discipline our desires.

Grace trains us to wait. "Training us to . . . [wait] for our blessed hope, the appearing of the glory of our great God and Savior Jesus Christ" (2:13). Before grace we had no eternal hope and therefore impatiently chased after all the glitter and gold of this world. But after God's meritless mercy possessed us, we possessed the hope of seeing the glory of our great God and Savior, Jesus Christ, for which we now patiently wait with expectation.

Grace trains us to be owned. It reminds us that Jesus "gave himself for us to redeem us from all lawlessness and to purify for himself a people for his own possession" (2:14). Before grace, we claimed ownership of ourselves. But grace loosens our grip on our lives by showing us how Christ let go of his own life for us to purchase us as his own.

Grace trains us to be zealous. It trains us to be "zealous for good works" (2:14). Previously, we had little or no desire for good works. But grace trains us to boil over with passion to do good works that please God.

Grace costs nothing but demands everything.

Changing Our Story with God's Story

Grace motivates us; grace keeps us accountable; grace guides us; grace keeps us going; and above all, unlike every other trainer, grace is free! No wonder Paul instructs Titus to work on enrolling others: "Declare these things; exhort and rebuke with all authority. Let no one disregard you" (2:15).

Summary: How can we get a spiritual trainer? *Get saved by grace to be trained by grace for spiritual growth and strength.*

Question: Which spiritual muscle is grace training in you?

Prayer: Strong Trainer, thank you for saving and training me by grace. Continue to develop me so that I consistently grow in good character and do good works.

If we'll be perfectly changed in heaven, then we can be partially changed on earth.

 Hear God's Story | Change Your Story | Tell the Story | Change Others' Stories

48

Can People Change?

TITUS 3:1–7

"He'll never change. He is who he is." Have you ever said that? Have you ever thought that about a friend, a colleague, a son, a husband, a fellow Christian? It's tempting at times, isn't it? No matter how much advice, counseling, help, or resources are offered, some people just remain stuck. Past habits are still present habits, and they look like they will be future habits too. *Are there some Christians who just can't change?*

In the previous chapter, Paul reminded Titus and his Cretan congregation of the need for grace-powered change. But did he have much hope for fundamental change in the Cretan Christians? Yes, definitely. Although he had already noted their deep national sin traits, in Titus 3:1–7 Paul articulates his hope that even these traits and characteristics could be changed.

The Worst Christians Can Change 3:1–2

Paul knew that the Cretans were rebellious, disobedient, lazy, gossipy, argumentative, harsh, and rude. But he urged Titus to "remind them to be submissive to rulers and authorities, to be obedient, to be ready for every good work, to speak evil of no one, to avoid quarreling, to be gentle, and to show perfect courtesy toward all people" (3:1–2). He didn't give up and say, "I agree with their poet that the Cretan character is unsalvageable." No, when grace appears, change appears even in the most ingrained characteristics.

If Cretans can change, then anyone can change.

"But no one is as hopeless as me."
No one was as hopeless as the apostle Paul.

The Apostle Paul Changed 3:3–6

Paul had strong hopes of change in the Cretans because he had seen big change in himself. If he could be changed, then anyone could. "For we ourselves were once foolish, disobedient, led astray, slaves to various passions and pleasures, passing our days in malice and envy, hated by others and hating one another" (3:3). That was in the past though. His present character is now wise, obedient, free, loving, and useful.

What changed? "But when the goodness and loving kindness of God our Savior appeared, he saved us, not because of works done by us in righteousness, but according to his own mercy, by the washing of regeneration and renewal of the Holy Spirit, whom he poured out on us richly through Jesus Christ our Savior" (3:4–6).

If Paul could be changed, then anyone can be changed.

"How much change can I hope for?"
Hope for full and forever change.

We Will Be Changed 3:7

Paul had hope not only of change in this life but of a changed eternal life: "So that being justified by his grace we might become heirs according to the hope of eternal life" (3:7). Being justified by grace meant he would be glorified by grace too. The work that grace began in justification is continued in sanctification, and will be perfected in glorification.

What a change that will be when we leave behind this life and inherit eternal life. We shall be changed in a moment, in the twinkling of an eye, into the likeness of Christ (1 Cor. 15:52). We will immediately be made perfect in holiness. If God can make us perfect so quickly at the end, can he not change us even a little in the here and now? Of course he can.

If we'll be perfectly changed in heaven,
then we can be partially changed on earth.

Changing Our Story with God's Story

The StoryChanger can change the most unchangeable story. If we know the StoryChanger, then we can know hope for others and for ourselves.

Summary: Are there some Christians who just can't change? *Hope for change in every Christian because God can change the worst Christians, the apostle Paul, and ourselves.*

Question: What about your own grace-change encourages you about the possibility of grace change in others?

Prayer: God of All Grace and of All Change, I have hope in your power to change because you have changed me and will continue to change me. Change others in the same way your grace has changed me.

Some will argue themselves right into hell.

 Hear God's Story | Change Your Story | Tell the Story | Change Others' Stories

49

Profit and Loss

TITUS 3:8–11

A friend once showed me something derogatory that another Christian pastor had written about me on the internet. For the next few hours, I plotted my revenge. I came up with so many zingers and one-liners that I thought I could be the next Jerry Seinfeld.

But as the Holy Spirit calmed my unholy spirit, I began to reason with myself: "Nothing you say will have any effect. You'll just be drawn in deeper and deeper. You'll lose more than you gain. It will spiral out of control. Pray for him, and trust the Lord with your reputation."

So I did, and a few hours later I began writing this chapter about how much we lose through engaging the foolish arguments of foolish arguers. *How much do we lose when we get drawn into internet arguments?* In Titus 3:8–10, Paul points to the profit of good works before turning to the unprofitability of foolish arguments.

Good Works Grow Spiritual Profit 3:8

Approaching the end of his short letter to Titus, Paul asserted the trustworthiness of what he wrote and therefore urged Titus to "insist on these things" (3:8). Titus was not left to decide what to do with Paul's teaching. It was not "take it or leave it," but "take it and insist on it."

Why? "So that those who have believed in God may be careful to devote themselves to good works. These things are excellent and profitable for people" (3:8). If faith was spiritual capital, then good works were the spiritual return on the investment.

As with any investment, believers are to be careful to devote themselves to ensuring a good return on investment. They are to audit their faith by a valuation of their good works to ensure spiritual profitability.

Good works are gold works.

"If that's the way to spiritual profit, what's the way to spiritual loss?" Foolish arguments.

Foolish Arguments Lose Spiritual Profit 3:9–11

The worst investment you will ever make is spending time and thought on the foolish arguments of foolish arguers, which is why Paul urges us to avoid them.

"But avoid foolish controversies, genealogies, dissensions, and quarrels about the law, for they are unprofitable and worthless" (3:9). If you want to put a hole in your spiritual wallet, engage in foolish arguments. You'll end up bankrupt with no assets.

But we're to do more than simply avoid foolish arguments. We're to avoid foolish arguers: "As for a person who stirs up division, after warning him once and then twice, have nothing more to do with him, knowing that such a person is warped and sinful; he is self-condemned" (3:10–11).

I recently did this on Facebook. A pastor had started trolling everything I posted, leaving snarky comments that diverted attention away from what I posted, and embroiling people in defending me or piling on to me.

I eventually thought, "I wouldn't let this divisive person in my house, so why should I let him on my social media page? I decided to block him, and my social media page returned to a source of profit rather than loss. I didn't have a verse for this at the time. I do now.

But I didn't just block him; I prayed for him and still do, because I don't want him to end up at the end of his life realizing he had condemned himself to everlasting poverty.

Some will argue themselves right into hell.

Changing Our Story with God's Story

Jesus modeled this perfectly on this earth. There were times when he blocked foolish arguers and ignored their questions, so that he could invest himself in good works.

Summary: How much do we lose when we get drawn into internet arguments? *Invest in good works rather than foolish arguments to build spiritual profit rather than suffer spiritual loss.*

Question: How can you grow your spiritual profit and reduce your losses?

Prayer: Rich God, invest in me with your grace and help me to invest in others with good works so that I can give you a good return on your investment.

**Salvation is not about doing our best.
But service is about doing our best.**

 Hear God's Story | Change Your Story | Tell the Story | Change Others' Stories

50

Do Your Best

TITUS 3:12–15

"Do your best" is the worst possible answer to the question, "What must I do to be saved?" Our best is not good enough and never can be. The only way to be saved is by grace through faith in Christ, not by doing our best.

However, "Do your best" is a great answer to the question, *"How should I serve?"* If that sounds heretical to you, then read Titus 3:12–15, where the apostle of grace tells those saved by grace to do their best when it comes to service. But, as we'll also see, we cannot do our best apart from grace.

Do Your Best 3:12–15

Paul urged Titus to do his best in three specific areas. First, he was to do his best to come and visit him: "When I send Artemas or Tychicus to you, do your best to come to me at Nicopolis, for I have decided to spend the winter there" (3:12).

Second, he was to do his best to send other Christians to him: "Do your best to speed Zenas the lawyer and Apollos on their way; see that they lack nothing" (3:13).

Third, Titus was to do his best to tell other Christians to do their best when it came to good works: "And let our people learn to devote themselves to good works, so as to help cases of urgent need, and not be unfruitful" (3:14). Devotion to good works indicates the level of commitment Paul expected of Titus and his congregation. Their devotional life included not only prayer but practice. In doing so, they were to prioritize urgent needs and care for others in such a way that would produce beautiful fruit.

Having urged Titus and the Christians to do their very best in various works and services, Paul then sent greetings to them: "All who are with me send greetings to you. Greet those who love us in the faith" (3:15).

Salvation is not about doing our best.
But service is about doing our best.

"So, do we start by grace alone, but then serve by just doing our best?" No, ultimately that's of grace also.

Do All by Grace 3:15

Just in case people might think Paul has renounced grace and returned to works, he closes his letter with "Grace be with you all" (3:15).

Throughout this letter to Titus, he has emphasized salvation by grace, which leads to good works, and he wants to make sure his last words point his readers back to grace as the source of all good works and words.

Paul has no hesitation about calling on God's people to exert themselves in God's service, to put in effort, labor, work, sweat, toil, and tears. But at the same time, he also points God's people to God's grace as the ultimate source of their energy and efforts. Paul knows that Titus, his congregation, and we today need both emphases: salvation by grace and sanctification by grace. God's people need to hear about God's sovereignty and human responsibility.

All is of grace. All is by grace.

Changing Our Story with God's Story

Many non-Christians often get confused about how a person is saved. When people come to faith, they recognize that it was all of grace not of works. However, once people are saved, they are called to work and serve with their best efforts that are derived from and by grace. This delicate balance is the key to people being saved and the saved being sanctified.

Paul finishes his three pastoral letters by reminding young Timothy and Titus, as well as all of us of a similar spirit, that by grace fear is to be replaced by courage.

Summary: How should I serve? *Do your best for God by the grace of God.*

Question: In what areas of Christian service can you do better?

Prayer: God of All Grace, may your grace save me apart from my best, and also empower me to serve you with my best.

TheStoryChanger.life

To keep changing your story with God's Story, visit www.thestorychanger.life for the latest news about more StoryChanger devotionals, to sign up for the StoryChanger newsletter, and to subscribe to the *The StoryChanger* podcast.

Also Available in the StoryChanger Devotional Series

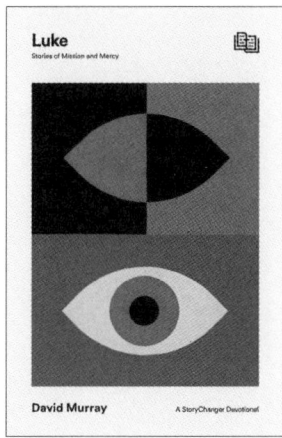

For more information, visit **crossway.org**.